PERGAMON INTERNATIONAL LIBRARY
of Science, Technology, Engineering and Social Studies

*The 1000-volume original paperback library in aid of education,
industrial training and the enjoyment of leisure*

Publisher: Robert Maxwell, M.C.

THE STATE
OF THE PLANET

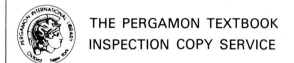

Other Titles of Interest

BALASSA, B.
Policy Reform in Developing Countries

BHALLA, A.
Towards Global Action for Appropriate Technology

BOTKIN, J. *et al.*
No Limits to Learning: Bridging the Human Gap

ECKHOLM, E.
Losing Ground: Environmental Stress and World Food Prospects

FITZGERALD, R.
Human Needs and Politics

JOLLY, R.
Disarmament and World Development

MENON, B.
Global Dialogue: The New International Economic Order

PECCEI, A.
The Human Quality

SINHA, R. and DRABEK, A.
The World Food Problem: Consensus and Conflict

TICKELL, C.
Climatic Change and World Affairs

WENK, E.
Margins for Survival: Overcoming Political Limits in Steering Technology

WIENER, A.
Magnificent Myth: Patterns of Control in Post-Industrial Society

THE STATE
OF THE PLANET

A REPORT PREPARED FOR THE INTERNATIONAL FEDERATION
OF INSTITUTES FOR ADVANCED STUDY (IFIAS), STOCKHOLM

By

ALEXANDER KING

Chairman of IFIAS

PERGAMON PRESS
OXFORD · NEW YORK · TORONTO · SYDNEY · PARIS · FRANKFURT

U.K.	Pergamon Press Ltd., Headington Hill Hall, Oxford OX3 0BW, England
U.S.A.	Pergamon Press Inc., Maxwell House, Fairview Park, Elmsford, New York 10523, U.S.A.
CANADA	Pergamon of Canada, Suite 104, 150 Consumers Road, Willowdale, Ontario M2J 1P9, Canada
AUSTRALIA	Pergamon Press (Aust.) Pty. Ltd., P.O. Box 544, Potts Point, N.S.W. 2011, Australia
FRANCE	Pergamon Press SARL, 24 rue des Ecoles, 75240 Paris, Cedex 05, France
FEDERAL REPUBLIC OF GERMANY	Pergamon Press GmbH, 6242 Kronberg-Taunus, Pferdstrasse 1, Federal Republic of Germany

British Library Cataloguing in Publication Data

International Federation of Institutes for
Advanced Study
The state of the planet.
1. Science - Social aspects
2. Technological innovations - Social aspects
I. Title   II. King, A.
301.24'3   Q175.5   79-40069

ISBN 0 08 024717 2 (Hardcover)
ISBN 0 08 024716 4 (Flexicover)

Opinions expressed in this publication do not necessarily reflect the views of IFIAS' Member Institutes or Board of Trustees.

Printed in Great Britain by A. Wheaton & Co. Ltd., Exeter

Contents

Preface to the Second Edition

The first edition of this brief discussion of world problems was published in a variety of languages and in two forms—the full text intended for informed members of the public, decision-makers, etc., and a shorter, more popular edition, lavishly illustrated, for schools and for more general readers. For reasons beyond the control of IFIAS, no edition in English was available, although a large number of mimeographed copies were distributed.

In the two years which have passed, it is difficult to see much improvement in the world situation. Most of the problems outlined have become aggravated: economic doubts have not been stilled, although economic growth is still the explicit objective of most countries; environmental uncertainties still persist, while their relevance to decision-making has become clearer; population trends have modified marginally; and the proportion of world resources devoted to armaments has increased still further. However, there is one important indication which kindles optimism, namely a substantial increase in public awareness of the problems in many parts of the world, expressed in books, newspaper and magazine articles, television programmes and debates.

One mark of this increasing interest was the decision of the United Nations to convene a World Conference on Science and Technology for Development, which was held in Vienna in August 1979. This important meeting, preparations for which took place in all the countries of the world, was mainly focused on the problems of development of the Third World and reduction in the disparities between the rich and the poor, but it was also broadly concerned with the longer-term world issues. It was preceded by an unofficial conference, held in Singapore in January 1979, with which IFIAS was associated, organized on behalf of the international science community, at which the concern of the community was demonstrated, some of the major problems analysed, and the will of the scientists expressed, to contribute to the maximum extent towards their solution.

In view of these trends and events IFIAS presents an updated version of its *State of the Planet* Report in the hope that it may add to the further increase in understanding of the problems which beset contemporary society.

I am grateful for the help of many friends in the IFIAS family for comments on various aspects of the compilation and especially to Dr Sam Nilsson, the Director of IFIAS who has worked with me and provided most of the tables and figures in the volume.

Paris and Stockholm
December 1979

Alexander King
Chairman, IFIAS Board of Trustees

Preface to the First Edition

In September 1969 a meeting took place in Stockholm on the initiative of the Nobel Foundation, which brought together some thirty scholars, world authorities from a broad spectrum of the arts and sciences, to discuss the human predicament in a world where development, including that of science, appeared to be running out of control. Despite the variety of disciplines, nationalities and ideologies represented, a high level of communication between the participants was established and a reassessment of the place of scientific and technological development in world society took place. It was the common conviction that scientific development has, and will still more in the future, induce changes in human values in most societies and that the complex problems of contemporary society can only be approached intelligently by the combined attack of many disciplines; yet the extension of human knowledge through research comes mainly from an ever deeper penetration within single disciplines, from ever greater specialization.

The Chairman of the symposium, Arne Tiselius, himself a Nobel Laureate, was profoundly impressed by the need to evolve scientific thinking in a more intimate understanding of human needs and to encourage a multidisciplinary attack on the great problems of mankind. At his instigation and with the support of the Nobel and Rockefeller Foundations, the International Federation of Institutes of Advanced Study (IFIAS) was created, with its small secretariat in the Nobel House in Stockholm, bringing together a limited number, at present twenty-two, specialized institutes of high quality, concerned with a wide variety of specializations, to promote and operate multidisciplinary research projects on major world problems. This young organization has proved to be particularly vigorous and has already launched a series of important studies on world problems, achieving harmonious working between scientists of diverse specializations and nationality.

At the 1974 meeting of the IFIAS Board of Trustees, it was proposed and generally agreed that the Chairman be invited to prepare a brief report on "the state of the Planet" which, if it appeared to be sufficient and appropriate, would be disseminated widely. This I have attempted to do and it is presented for the attention of the general public and especially of decision makers.

At first sight, such an effort may appear to be excessively ambitious and even pretentious. However, there are strong reasons why such an attempt should be made. The growing number of global problems, their complexity and interaction, the rapidity of change—political, social, economic, technological and cultural—increasing recognition that there must exist both inner and outer levels to human activity and human consumption: these and many other trends are so disturbing and so interconnected that there is urgent need to review them in their totality and to draw widespread attention to their significance for our own lives and those of our children. It is desirable therefore that some group should shoulder the responsibility and report from time to time on "the state of the Planet", on the evolution of the global problems, and on measures taken to face them.

Because of the global nature of the trends which we shall consider, it is too much to expect that individual governments, preoccupied as they are with immediate issues, will take the initiative to survey and prepare balance sheets of the world situation, let alone act on what they have learnt. By rights this should be the task of the United Nations, but that organization is itself too complex and too cumbersome and so constrained by conflicting political considerations, that it is unlikely to take on this burden, at least sufficiently quickly, despite the final pronouncement of its late Secretary General, U. Thant. It should be recognized, however, that the United Nations Institute for Training and Research (UNITAR), through its Commission on the Future, is moving in this direction.

IFIAS, although a small and comparatively obscure organization, seems to be well placed to take on this task, even if only in a preliminary way and, initially at least, in a fractional and incomplete manner. The Federation, conceived and constituted as a network of highly competent institutes of research in all continents of the world, lacking political aims and constraints and basically concerned with investigating global problems in a multidisciplinary perspective, is in a position to receive inputs from a wide variety of scientific, economic, social and cultural systems, to analyse these objectively and to subject its analysis of world problems to the scrutiny of scholars from many fields. IFIAS seems therefore a suitable body which might move towards a "world watch" and present the changing balance of dangers and new possibilities. The inadequacies of IFIAS for this purpose are also recognized, arising mainly from the incomplete coverage of world intellec-

tual activity of the member institutes. It is beyond our capacity, at least for the present, to present a review of the main geopolitical events of the times or to provide an acceptable analysis of the present world economic trends and their significance for future world development. The present report, therefore, is restricted to those aspects of the world *problématique* which are, by their nature, open to scientific scrutiny in the larger sense of the word *Science, Wissenschaft* or *Nauk,* which are the Federation's own concern.

There is little in the way of new facts or scientific discovery reported here. Indeed many of the individual topics have been described before and often in greater depth by individual experts. Its value resides in the attempt to provide an over-all perspective of the situation, to give a reasonable statement with regard to each of the topics treated, to stress the interconnections and thus provide a picture of synthesis. Some will find the report somewhat pessimistic; others who have read the manuscript feel that it may not stress the dangers strongly enough. Its pessimism, of course, reflects to some extent the value judgements of its compiler, but the reader should remember that it concerns itself with the problems facing humanity, rather than with its achievements, just as when seeking medical advice, attention is given to what is wrong and not to what is functioning normally.

I have received great assistance from a wide variety of people who read the first draft and who responded with constructive criticism, not least the directors of most of the IFIAS Institutes. I am particularly indebted to Dr. Sam Nilsson, our Executive Secretary, for his ideas throughout, to Dr. Stephen H. Schneider of NCAR in the USA whose forthcoming book *The Genesis Strategy* covers much of the same ground, although mainly from a climatological point of view, to Professor Dennis Gabor in UK and to Professor N. Buras of the Technion, Haifa, who substantially rewrote the section on water resources. The report should not be taken as a formally agreed declaration of IFIAS, although it has the general concensus of the member institutes. I am solely responsible for its inadequacies.

Paris, January 1976   Alexander King
                  Chairman, IFIAS Board of Trustees

CHAPTER 1

The Darkest Shadows

Amongst the multitudinous and varied problems facing world societies today, we believe that the most urgent and the most important for a harmonious development of world societies, hinges on our ability to feed, clothe, house, educate and provide decent conditions of health and employment to the burgeoning population of the earth. The United Nations forecasts that the population of the world will double in little more than thirty years. Already an extra million persons are added to the population about every four-and-a-half days, or about 80 million extra mouths to feed each year. In view of the present demographic structure, with a very low average age due to recent growth, this doubling will involve a threefold increase in the global work force.

The problems of rapid population increase cannot be dissociated from those of the excessive disparities between the rich and the poor countries of the world—the so-called North/South question. These disparities, already intolerable, are still growing and are a serious threat to world harmony as well as a moral challenge to the rich nations, in consequence of the extensive misery and wastage involved. The greatest part of the expected population increase takes place in countries already poor and with many of their citizens undernourished and underemployed. In Table 1 and Fig. 1 are given two projections of the population in different regions from 1977 and 1974 respectively.

It has taken centuries to build up the world infrastructure which serves the present population—the houses, schools, transportation systems, production and distribution networks and many other elements, not least important of which are the means to grow, preserve and distribute food. Can we, in fact, hope to duplicate these massive structures in thirty short years? If so, what will be the cost in terms of materials and energy, of the provision of capital and skills and also the impact on the environment, investment, trade, balance of payment, internal social situation and general development of every nation in the world? If not, what will be the cost in economic, social, and political terms and, above all, in human suffering and despair? Yet, despite the 1974 Conference of the United Nations on World Population and a general, growing concern with these problems, there is little concrete evidence that serious preparations are being made to receive decently, this new multitude of world citizens, which is, as it were, already standing in the wings ready to march on to the stage.

TABLE 1

Estimates and Projections of Total Population and the Related Growth Rates—World and Regions—1960-2000

Region	Total population (millions)							Average annual growth rates (per cent)					
	1960	1965	1970	1975	1980	1990	2000	1960-1965	1965-1970	1970-1975	1975-1980	1980-1990	1990-2000
Developed Market Economies	650.2	690.8	724.4	757.1	791.2	859.8	922.8	1.2	1.0	0.9	0.9	0.8	0.7
North America	198.6	213.9	226.3	236.7	248.7	275.0	296.0	1.5	1.1	0.9	1.0	1.0	0.7
Western Europe	326.8	343.0	354.0	364.3	374.1	394.4	413.8	1.0	0.6	0.6	0.5	0.5	0.5
Oceania	12.7	14.0	15.4	16.8	18.4	21.5	24.5	2.0	1.9	1.8	1.8	1.6	1.3
Other Developed Market Economies	112.1	119.8	128.8	139.2	150.0	168.9	188.4	1.3	1.5	1.6	1.5	1.2	1.1
Eastern Europe and USSR	312.7	332.9	347.9	363.8	380.6	412.9	440.7	1.3	0.9	0.9	0.9	0.8	0.7
ALL DEVELOPED COUNTRIES	962.9	1023.7	1072.3	1120.9	1171.8	1272.7	1363.5	1.2	0.9	0.9	0.9	0.8	0.7
Developing Market Economies	1323.1	1500.4	1704.9	1939.5	2217.6	2878.8	3623.5	2.5	2.6	2.6	2.7	2.6	2.3
Africa	219.4	246.3	279.3	318.8	366.7	491.8	657.9	2.3	2.5	2.7	2.8	3.0	3.0
Latin America	215.6	247.3	283.0	324.1	371.6	385.6	619.9	2.8	2.7	2.7	2.8	2.7	2.5
Near East	130.4	148.3	169.9	195.0	224.8	297.4	380.4	2.6	2.7	2.8	2.9	2.8	2.5
Far East	754.6	854.8	968.7	1097.0	1249.3	1597.3	1956.9	2.5	2.5	2.5	2.6	2.5	2.1
Other Developing Market Economies	3.2	3.6	4.0	4.6	5.2	6.7	8.3	2.5	2.5	2.5	2.6	2.6	2.2
Asian Centrally Planned Economies	701.5	764.5	833.1	907.7	985.2	1129.7	1269.7	1.7	1.7	1.7	1.7	1.4	1.2
ALL DEVELOPING COUNTRIES	2024.6	2264.9	2538.0	2847.2	3202.8	4008.5	4893.2	2.3	2.3	2.3	2.4	2.3	2.0
WORLD	2987.5	3288.6	3610.4	3968.1	4374.6	5281.2	6256.7	1.9	1.9	1.9	2.0	1.9	1.7

Note: The above regional aggregates are based on the country by country estimates and projections of the population prepared by the United Nations. For details regarding the methods and assumptions underlying the projections please see *World Population Prospects as Assessed in 1973, Population Studies* No. 60, ST/ESA/Ser.A/60, United Nations, New York, 1977.

Source: The Fourth World Food Survey, FAO 1977

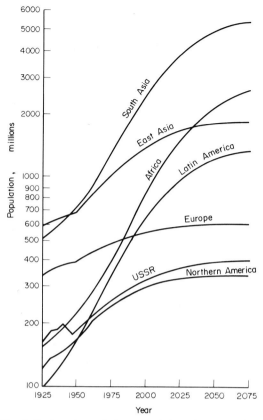

Fig. 1. Projected population growth in major areas of the world, 1925-2075, according to the UN medium variant of long-range projections, charted on a logarithmic scale. (From *Concise report on the world population situation 1970-1975 and its long-range implications,* United Nations, 1974.)

Moreover, there are as yet few signs that world leadership has a clear consciousness of the immensity of the impending problems both to the developing and to the developed countries.

In the industrialized countries, it is too often assumed that the problems of development and of the population explosion in many parts of the world are essentially difficulties of the Third World countries as such, with too little recognition of the repercussions which the evolution of these problems could have on the presently industrialized and affluent parts of the world. Development aid is seen, if not by the informed minority in the developed world, certainly by the general population, as a form of charity rather than as a matter of long term self-interest and a necessity for global stability. Despite the discussions at the United Nations of the New International Economic Order, NIEO, there is still an absence of a firm resolve to move towards solutions that will be acceptable to the diverse societies of the world.

We do not believe, however, that the situation is hopeless, although it will become quickly more menacing the longer the delay in facing it. There are innumerable technical possibilities of increasing the food availability, so that spectacular strides could be taken towards solving the immediate problem of feeding the world. These, however, will not be actualized unless a political will is generated, and in order to do so world opinion must be alerted to the gravity of the problem, together with the understanding of its wide implications.

Related to the problems of population and Third World Development are those of maintaining ample supplies of reasonably cheap energy, a subject to which we shall refer later in more detail. Feeding growing populations has depended substantially on mechanized agriculture, which in turn requires chemical fertilizer for high productivity, and this depends on the availability of petroleum. The provision of food and other basic needs in the future will demand a considerable increase in the provision of energy, especially in the less developed countries, for example for the manufacture of fertilizers, agricultural machinery, transportation of food, desalination of water and many other purposes. We are in a period of considerable price increase in energy sources and it will probably be several decades before non-traditional energy sources become sufficiently available; indeed, massive and coordinated research effort in this direction has hardly begun and, with the very long lead time in scientific research and technological development, to say nothing of that for capital accumulation and the construction of the very large manufacturing facilities which will be necessary, this could be a dangerous brake on food production.

It can be argued, of course, that there is already sufficient or nearly sufficient energy available in the world to meet reasonable human needs, but it is rather the profligate use of energy for unnecessary purposes which creates the difficulty. However, redistribution of what energy we have would entail drastic changes in life-style in the industrialized countries and could not take place quickly enough to meet the needs of a rising world population. Despite the present affluent abundance of energy, its future scarcity in the market place is likely to become one of the most fundamental problems of the next thirty years. With abundant energy, food can be produced and ways found to substitute for scarce materials of all kinds. Eventually sufficient, and clean, energy can be provided, but during the next few decades, which coincide with the population explosion, the difficulties will be great.

There is likely to be, then, a difficult transition period, beginning in the 1980s and lasting for several decades until the new forms of energy are available in sufficient quantities and until the world population is on the way to stabilization. Amongst other problems will be that of providing the capital to extend the infrastructure of the world for a doubled population and at the same time to renew the energy system. In the next chapter we shall discuss some of the features of the transition.

The inevitability of massive population increase, coupled with the long lead time of possible means to meet it leads us to express our conviction *that the complex of problems involved in the provision of food and other necessities, together with that of reducing the North/South disparities as well as the related energy problems, constitutes the most immediate menace of the global issues.* Widespread recognition of this, the generation of political will to move quickly to solutions, and a recognition of the inevitable time lag in the implementation of plans and policies is the primary need.

We are aware, of course, of the many other serious problems, including above all the threat of nuclear annihilation. Some of them seem to be more immediately urgent, such as the need to curb inflation, the provision of employment and the reform of the monetary system; but from the point of view of the survival of society and continued planetary stability, even these are overshadowed by the consequences of inevitable population growth.

CHAPTER 2

World Society in Transition

It is exceedingly difficult at any point in time to identify and understand the major trends of society and to foresee its future form—matters which seem so obvious when looked back at in later years. This is particularly so in the present situation of rapid change—political, social, economic and technological—especially in view of uncertainty with regard to the value shifts of society and its constituent individuals. In this chapter we shall try to indicate some of the present world trends in the light of past evolution, in an attempt to identify some of the issues which society will have to face.

1. GROWTH AND TECHNOLOGY

For the last 200-300 years Western civilization has been riding on the crest of a gigantic wave of material growth which has seemed to carry it constantly forward and upward. This has been achieved in the light of the eighteenth century concept of progress, that man could improve his world and his future indefinitely. It has also been favoured by the potentialities which flowed, at first slowly and latterly in a torrent, from the Baconian approach of experimental science. It appeared that man's future could only be limited by his intrinsic ability and ingenuity. These have been the centuries of "progress", but unfortunately such progress has been predominantly material and has not been compensated by a corresponding growth of man's other faculties. There is, indeed, little evidence to suggest that human wisdom has evolved and deepened perceptibly over the last 3000 years, or that man has acquired fundamentally new and more profound insights into his own nature and his place in the universe.

The point of take-off in this curve of material growth was the industrial revolution which, through the steam engine, multiplied the power at the disposal of individual men and opened up the possibility of seemingly indefinite expansion of production. It should be remembered that the fathers of the industrial revolution in their optimism and enthusiasm saw in this and in the vistas opened up by the new scientific knowledge the prospect of universal abolition of poverty and the entry into a golden age. A second impulse came a century later when the content of the scientific disciplines filled up to the extent that they formed the basis for a systematic, sophisticated and ever more powerful technology, gradually replacing the empirical invention of the earlier part of the growth period. The availability of cheap energy encouraged the use of mechanization and automation and favoured the stimulation of increased manpower productivity, i.e. ever increasing production *per capita*. All this inevitably meant that innovation in technology was of the high capital and high energy intensive type. Unemployment, which was greatly feared at the early stages, was largely avoided by the continuous expansion of the total production effort and the opening up of new markets and hence of new jobs; in fact, in some of the European countries, despite high manpower productivity, it has only been possible to maintain expansion through the import of millions of foreign workers from less industrialized countries.

2. GROWTH FOR GROWTH'S SAKE

Gradually it became clear that the system could only keep running through continuous expansion; the growth mania meant, therefore, that existing markets had to keep on expanding and new ones had to be opened up; insidiously the persuasion industry came into being, using the media to stimulate demand and consumption, often valuable in meeting real needs, but more often artificial in creating inessential demands, as the luxuries of the previous decade became the accepted necessities of the next, and involving enormous and wasteful use of materials and energy, with vicious components such as those of planned obsolescence or the deliberate reduction of the useful life of appliances.

Decade after decade of continuous growth has accustomed people in the industrialized countries to expect an equally continuous increase in take-home wages, in welfare amenities and in material possessions, although the extent to which former luxuries have become necessities makes them feel still deprived. One might have expected that an approach to saturation would be appearing, for there must be a limit to the number of material possessions the individual can usefully enjoy. There is,

however, little sign of this, despite plenty of evidence of the near saturation of cities and roads, air and water with the products and by-products of our material bonanza.

Economic growth, then, became the accepted yardstick of material progress. Its measure, increase in the Gross National Product (GNP), was eagerly followed, and comparisons of the prosperity levels of the different nations in terms of their GNP were presented as a sort of football league table, giving great satisfaction to the leaders and a spur to those at the bottom of the league. For a period, growth seemed to have become an end in itself, rather than the means of providing the resources for the achievement of the too vaguely formulated aims of society.

However, despite this strong performance poverty remains widespread. More than 700 million people still live in absolute poverty, defined as income per head of $200 or less per year. This amounts to almost 40% of the Third World's population. Furthermore, the number of poor, underemployed, malnourished, and illiterate people has risen over the years.

Behind the statistical figures of GNP *per capita* lies another reality of which the numbers in Table 2 below speak. Of the world's poor in 1976 in a total population of 4000 million the following holds:

TABLE 2

Undernourished (i.e. below suggested calorie/protein levels)	570 million
Adults illiterate	800 million
Children not enrolled in school	250 million
With no access to effective medical care	1,500 million
With less than $90 income per year	1,300 million
With life expectancy below 60 years	1,700 million
With inadequate housing	1,030 million

Source: John McHale and Magda Cordell McHale, *Basic Human Needs,* Transaction Books, New Brunswick, N.J., 1978.

3. GROWTH AND DISPARITY

Great as have been the material benefits of economic growth, there has been an increasing realization that the gains have been unfairly distributed. The early dreams of abolishing poverty have not come true and disequity and great disparity in the distribution of wealth, both within and between countries, constitute one of the other great issues of the contemporary world. In the rich, industrialized countries there has, of course, been considerable social reform and the institution of welfare systems and greater educational opportunity. Furthermore, income inequality has been greatly reduced in consequence of technological progress, which in increasing manpower productivity has also increased the price of labour. In addition, ownership of capital has become more dispersed; thus the grosser forms of poverty and exploitation have been eradicated.

However, new forms of poverty, some of them somewhat artificial, have appeared and new tensions have arisen as expectations of prosperity have increased and the unwanted side effects of technology and industrialization have become more and more evident. Many feel that the work ethic, which played such an important role in the earlier stages of industrialization, seems to be evaporating as welfare measures have lessened the struggle for existence, while alienation of a proportion of the population grows as a result of the impersonality of urban life and the loss of its quality or in the drabness of existence in faceless suburbs. Excessive mechanization and line production methods have removed the satisfaction of work. Higher average *per capita* income simply does not equate with what many consider to be quality of life.

The disparities in wealth between the rich and the poor countries are more marked and potentially more menacing. At first sight, growth rates in the Third World are impressive and a few countries not particularly well endowed with natural resources, including Korea, Taiwan, Singapore and Hong Kong, have prospered well, to the extent that their exported manufactures cause some disquiet in the main, industrialized countries. During the decades of the 50s and 60s, the developing countries in Africa, Latin America and Asia have achieved an average growth rate of about 5% per annum. This compares favourably with the growth record of the industrialized world, but it starts from a very low base line and much of the new wealth created finds its way to the already well-to-do as a result of inequity of the social system in many countries, so that the great masses have benefited but little from technology transfer, improved agriculture and the in-flow of aid capital and loans. Furthermore, the *per capita* gain in national income was reduced to about 2½% in many places through population increase, while substantial purchases of military equipment have further reduced the benefits of growth. It is thus misleading to assess the situation simply in terms of GNP as the evidence of poverty in Table 2 indicates. Thus in the 1970s, more people than ever seem to be underprivileged on practically all the indicators of poverty.

Recognition of the weight of the internal disequities has given rise of late to a focus of attention on the urgency of satisfying the fundamental needs of every inhabitant of the planet, to make possible at least a life of modest human dignity and as a basis for further development. This concept cannot be approached through the indiscriminate terms of GNP growth but stresses the importance of people and their potentialities. The *basic human needs strategy* is usually defined in terms of supplying universally an adequate level of nutrition, shelter and clothing, the provision of employment, education and health services, access to information and security of the person. Although these elements are basic to all people in all countries, the required levels and qualities will vary somewhat according to the environment and the culture and it is important that they should be determined specifically in the case of each nation and not dictated centrally from New York or elsewhere.

The promotion of basic human needs is essentially a response to recognition of the unfair distribution of wealth *within* a country and thus necessarily involves plans and policies to favour social change, including taxation, access to education and land reform, and must be channelled to many points in the national strategy. It must be recognized, therefore, that although such an approach can be widely accepted on equity grounds and those of social stability, it is bound to meet some internal resistance and could in some cases appear, initially at least, to run counter to the long established traditions. Inevitably, the elites of some countries must see it as a threat to the existing patterns of power as well as their relative wealth.

4. THE GENERALIZATION OF EXPECTATIONS

One consequence of scientific and technological development with world-wide repercussions has been the introduction of modern systems of communication and transportation and this has led rapidly, first to the generalization of information throughout the world and then to that of expectations. Remote communities in India receive educational materials via an American satellite; events taking place almost everywhere on the planet are made known immediately and universally. People in remote and impoverished parts of the world have, for the first time, a visual, although often distorted, picture of how the other half lives. An apparently endless vista of wealth arising from technology and of new and confusing life styles is projected, which seems to be unaware or uncaring for the majority of mankind, contrasting starkly with local misery, lack of opportunity and immobility.

One dubious consequence of the generalization of expectations lies in the nature of the expectations. The dramatic achievements of Western, growth-oriented civilization, whatever its drawbacks, and the appeal of material possessions and material well-being are so great that many countries in earlier stages of development seem bent on emulating the West, of constructing industrialized societies based on the same processes which have already produced so much wealth and so much distress, attempting to bridge the gap and in the process repeating the mistakes. In fact, despite the many declarations of political leaders throughout the world that their countries must find their own ways and develop in terms of their own values and cultural patterns, the Western, material way of life is quickly, if insidiously, penetrating into most cultures and societies, producing local tensions and augmenting local disparities. Too often the result for the individual is an exchange of rural subsistence and underemployment for urban misery and unemployment.

There is, indeed, a certain disenchantment in many countries, with the Western model of development, hitherto assumed in the aid programmes to be universally applicable and desirable. For one thing, there is evidence that those societies which have cultivated technological development and economic growth most successfully have achieved material success at the cost of accumulating social problems, including persistent unemployment, crime, drug addiction, alienation and environmental deterioration, amongst the many unwanted side-effects of technological development and indiscriminate growth. On the other side, opinion has grown in some of the less developed countries that imported technology has had some unfavourable impacts on local economies and on cultural traditions. Modern methods of mechanized farming and production methods have disturbed traditional ways of life and led to migration to the cities, thus replacing rural underemployment by urban employment. In many places there has been a distortion of consumption patterns, inducing new and unsuitable modes of living and personal behaviour which are seen as threats to traditional values and institutions. All in all, the situation seems to many to be one of diminishing cultural integrity and its replacement by new and foreign modes which are only partly integrated into the culture and accentuate the stratification of society. Meanwhile, there is a widening of the gap between rich and poor, between the countryside and the cities. Such reservations concerning the universal validity of the Western model are leading many people in the Third World to reassess the value of their own traditions and to consider alternative paths to development which are more distinctively their own. On the basis of a workshop held at Bellagio in 1975, IFIAS circulated a statement of the group, advocating the maintenance of cultural diversity in the development process.*

5. THE PROBLEMS OF CONTEMPORARY SOCIETY

By the middle of the 1960s, the industrialized countries were beginning to feel uncomfortable about their situation. The environmental problems were the first to become generally recognized by the public as a threat to the continuation of their way of life and growth. Technology, arising mainly in response to the profit motive rather than to meeting human needs, seemed to be producing unexpected and unwanted side effects. The environment appeared to be threatened with possibly irreversible changes, which might have disastrous effects on the climate and on many biological species, including possibly man. Ecological and conservationist movements sprang up every-

* Global Development: The End of Cultural Diversity?, IFIAS Statement from the Bellagio Workshop, *International Association* No. 8-9, 1976.

where, a few science-based, some fanatical, others irresponsible and distorting the facts, but all reflecting a deepening concern.

Then came the student troubles of 1967-68, which signalled a deep unrest and dissatisfaction with the workings of society in general and not merely a rejection of the traditional education system which was seen as preparing young people for life in a world which was fading away, rather than for the change and uncertainty of the future. This was but one sign of a general loss of confidence that societies and their leaders knew where they were going.

A few years later again the report to the Club of Rome on the *Limits to Growth* raised doubts as to the capacity of the earth to sustain growth for much longer. Depletion of raw materials, population growth, environmental contamination and increasing industrialization all seemed to be growing exponentially and interacting with each other to produce a situation which would be disastrous to the human race if it were allowed to continue. Despite all the shortcomings of this work and of the criticisms, both rational and hysterical, it had a resounding impact throughout the world and has given substance to a debate that was overdue and that continues unabated. Like all warnings of the kind, the dire conclusions of the *Limits to Growth* will never materialize. Indeed the authors stated explicitly that this would be so; if people were sufficiently alerted to the dangers, policies and practices would be changed to ensure this. Of course, the world is finite and many of its limits can be assessed but, as the Club of Rome itself stated, the material limits are unlikely to be reached; the real limits lie in front, and are political, economic, social, managerial, and finally reside within the intrinsic nature of man. The *Limits to Growth* has had two other major values; it has pointed out clearly the importance of the interactions and reinforcements of the difficulties and it has triggered off major researches into the nature of the world problems and their interactions, which will be much more sophisticated and useful to policy makers than the original effort.

Exhaustion of most of the raw materials valued by man may well lie far in the future and may be further delayed by substitution, technological advance and conservation through recycling. Nevertheless, the rapidly growing demand as a result of continuing economic growth will have many difficult consequences including price rises resulting from scarcity, as the energy requirements and ecological costs of using lower grade materials increase. While the population increase in the industrialized lands is much lower than in the developing countries, the fact that the former have energy and material requirements *per capita* between 20 and 40 times that of the latter means that quite small population rises in industrialized countries will have a proportionately much greater influence on the demand for energy and materials if present income disparities persist. (See Table 3.)

Then came the petroleum crisis of recent years, which gave a nasty jolt to the developed countries, which they found difficult to absorb. The growth wave has been propelled for many years on cheap energy, the indefinite continuation of which, while questioned by many experts, was tacitly assumed by the body politic and economic to be immutable. However, the chief victims of the abrupt pricing manoeuvres and oil embargo in 1974 were the millions of the poor of the world deprived of sufficient fertilizer and other petroleum based props to food productions.

6. SOME TRENDS AND ISSUES

Most of the problems which are now acquiring critical dimensions have been with us for a

TABLE 3
Energy Use and GNP in Selected Countries, 1973

Country	Annual energy consumption per capita (MJ)	Equivalent GNP per capita ($US)	MJ/$	Net imports of energy (% of consumption)*
United States	344,000	6200	55	11
Czechoslovakia	193,000	2870	67	19
East Germany	180,000	3000	60	22
Sweden	176,000	5910	30	90
United Kingdom	166,000	3060	54	47
West Germany	167,000	5320	31	50
Netherlands	175,000	4330	40	37
USSR	142,000	2030	70	NE†
Switzerland	108,000	6100	18	80
Japan	104,000	3630	29	98
New Zealand	92,900	3680	25	58
Argentina	55,000	1640	34	12
Mexico	39,000	890	44	3
China, People's Republic	16,300	270	60	2
Brazil	16,300	760	21	54
Egypt	8,500	250	34	NE
India	5,400	120	45	18
Indonesia	3,800	130	29	NE
Nigeria	1,900	210	9	NE

Note: Excludes wood, dung, agricultural residues, food.
*1971.   † NE = net exporter.
Sources: UN, *Statistical Yearbook*; World Bank, *Atlas*.

long time, even if only in embryo form. Thus pollution in the industrial ghettos of the last century and the "dark satanic mills" of William Blake were considerably worse than conditions today, but they were strictly localized. Today such effects have become generalized and to some extent globally generalized. It is necessary, therefore, to examine some of the current trends as a prelude to the understanding of the importance and potential menace of the associated problems. The following are a few of the most important, those already dealt with being described, *pro memoria,* only in title.

(1) Demographic Change

As we have seen (Chapter 1), the consequences of the population explosion on the one hand and of the differentials in fertility between different parts of the world will pose important problems to all nations in the future. It is important that each country should establish well-considered population policies, whether pro- or anti-natalist, and these should be elaborated in the light of the total world demographic evolution.

(2) Increase in the Scale of Human Activity

This arises partly as a result of greater numbers and partly from the increased demand *per capita* resulting from enhanced levels of affluence in a significant proportion of the world population, as a consequence of technologically based economic growth of recent years. This has entailed a great extension of governmental activity in many countries in fields hitherto left to the private sector and the forces of the market. In many instances, governments are ill equipped to deal with the new scale and complexity of national management, parliaments find it difficult to understand many of the technical problems involved and the swelling of the bureaucracy has taken decision-making far

from those who enjoy or suffer its consequences.

(3) Mounting Demands for Food, Energy and Materials

Increased numbers and *per capita* demands have put great pressure on the procurement of materials and energy in many countries such as Japan and those of Western Europe with flourishing industries but possessing few natural resources of their own and dependent, therefore, on imports from distant countries. The recent petroleum crisis demonstrated how precarious such supplies can be. Food demand is also growing and will rise rapidly with population increase and put further pressure on energy supply. There is also a fear that the indefinite expansion of demand will rapidly exhaust the most accessible and therefore cheapest of the world's mineral and fossil fuel reserves and that with scarcity, raw materials and energy will become exceedingly costly. A further uncertainty concerns the extent to which the planet will be able to absorb the waste products of the greatly increased activity without irreversible damage.

(4) The Armaments Race

Quite apart from its military implications, the maintenance of large military forces and the complicated technology of defence and attack represents an enormous consumption of resources: material, energy and human. It is said that about half of the scientists of the world are occupied with defence matters and are hence unavailable to tackle the problems of society or to uncover new knowledge for human understanding. In addition to the situation of the major powers, the build-up of armaments in the poorer countries, which has greatly increased in recent years, represents a substantial flow-back of wealth from the poor to the rich countries. (For further discussion, see Chapter 4.)

(5) Nuclear Proliferation

Apart from the relatively slow increase in the number of "nuclear" nations in the strictly military sense, the "horizontal" proliferation of nuclear materials as a result of the need, or apparent need, for nuclear power generation is increasing rapidly and is being encouraged by countries anxious to sell atomic reactors as a normal commercial export. It has unfortunately proved impossible as yet to decouple the peaceful from the military uses of radioactive materials and the prospects of doing so are remote, unless an extensive, and possibly oppressive, international control is enforced.

(6) The Fragility of Contemporary Societies

The prosperity of society today is based on technology and more and more the smooth running of countries and their cities depends on the efficient functioning of technical devices. Yet these are extremely vulnerable to disruption and their malfunctioning or breakdown could quickly paralyse a city or nation. Electricity cuts, especially if prolonged, are particularly to be feared since they would interfere with transportation, halt the elevators of tall buildings and cripple the computer and communication systems on which the functioning of society increasingly depends.

Political terrorism is also on the increase, as recent events in Germany and Italy have shown. Dissatisfaction with contemporary society has led to the emergence of small, determined and fanatical groups hoping to disrupt the workings of that society. The vulnerability of aircraft has already given rise to many hi-jackings, but this could easily be only an initial and relatively trivial manifestation of the trend, since many of the technical nerve centres are equally vulnerable. Attack, or threat of attack, on installations such as power stations, nuclear reactors, oil refineries, communication networks and the like are to be expected, to say nothing of the kidnapping of political leaders, industrialists and leaders of society—and eventually nuclear blackmail.

(7) Speed of Change

One of the features of today's world is the rapid rate of change—political, economic, social and technological. To many people this denotes insecurity and uncertainty. It necessitates a greater mobility than in the past and a capacity to adapt quickly to new conditions of life and work. It also suggests that the institutions of society should be conceived in a dynamic rather than a static sense. The management of change and uncertainty as well as of complexity is so far lacking in methodology.

(8) The Long- versus the Short-term Issues

It is an inbuilt human characteristic to put off until tomorrow what should be done today and this is just as true of governments as of individuals. In the democratic system it is particularly difficult to tackle the longer term problems which are seldom seen as important by the electorate. With an electoral system of about four years, both governments and opposition parties have to give priority to issues of the moment which are of concern to the voters and find it difficult to face up to longer term problems which may be much more fundamental. In former times this has probably mattered little since, with slower change, the longer term difficulties evolved but slowly. This is, however, no longer so. What was previously a problem which might become acute some 25 years later now tends to become so in a five to ten years' span. The result is a situation in which governments are overtaken by events and tend to react to them by emergency legislation to meet each crisis as it appears, and with little time or inclination of looking more deeply into the underlying issues and thus to stagger from crisis to crisis. Here again there is need for institutional innovation. In view of the global nature of many of the problems, this function of looking ahead and analysing the future problems before they become acute is necessary on a world scale and will eventually become a major task for the United Nations. Since the practical application of scientific advances is inherently a long process and the consequences are not always clear at the outset, this scanning process is particularly necessary with regard to the implications of scientific progress and to ensure that new plants and processes will be available when required. (For further discussion see Chapter 8.)

(9) The Global Problems

Hitherto, despite the importance of foreign trade and of military and political alliances, countries have been relatively self-sufficient and have felt themselves to be so and hence free and able to solve their own problems in their own way. Contagious inflation, balance of payments problems, monetary difficulties, unemployment, economic depression or boom—all of these and other aspects of national life are becoming progressively internationalized. Likewise the procurement needs for energy and raw materials, now required in such enormous quantities, are to a greater or lesser extent escaping the control of individual countries. Smaller countries in particular, even if economically and structurally strong, are relatively at the mercy of external forces and their power of independent action is considerably curtailed.

In addition to these politico-economic matters, we are now witnessing the emergence of a number of problems of a more technical nature which have to be recognized as inherently global in scope. Atmospheric or water pollution, for example, cannot be contained within political frontiers and methods of control can-

not be effective in many cases, on a country to country basis, without harmonization of standards and regulations, otherwise the industries of those countries will be penalized in international competition by those with a more lax approach. Furthermore, major works in a particular country such as the cutting down of tropical rain forests, diversion of rivers or the use of off-shore thermal currents, have a possible significant influence on the climate at great distances. The problems of the exploitation of the oceans and their beds are essentially international in character and are at present giving rise to difficult political negotiations. Attempts at rain-making or weather control are seen as "robbing Peter to pay Paul". These and many other matters are of essentially world-wide importance and are increasingly regarded in this light, yet the machinery for discussing, such as exists, is becoming increasingly politicized. Many of the global problems cannot be tackled on an individual country basis; and just because they are of concern to all, they tend to be the responsibility of none. "Tragedy of the Commons" was the title of the now classic article by Garrett Hardin *(Science Magazine)*. Such problems are, furthermore, generally discussed in terms of the opposing, short-term interests of the individual nations. From the point of view of our present concern, there is a very strong argument in favour of new, comprehensive arrangements to tackle the global issues, before they get out of hand.

(10) Climatic Uncertainty

A new uncertainty has been recognized in recent years, namely there seems to be a general, but erratic deterioration in world climate which could have deep implications for agriculture, energy demand and human settlement. Nothing can be said with certainty about future climatic conditions and the experts are far from unanimous as to the prospects. It does appear, however, that recent decades represent something approaching the optimum climate as far as agriculture is concerned and many of the climatologists think that we must expect a period of uncertainty with greater extremes of heat and cold, drought and flood. It is not clear as yet as to the extent which these trends can be attributed to human intervention, if at all. Nevertheless, the threat to the world's climate through heating-up as a consequence of the "greenhouse" effect, as increase in the carbon dioxide content of the air reaches sizeable proportions due to the burning of fossil fuels, or partial destruction of the ozone layer, is serious but uncertain. We shall return to this problem later. (See Chapter 5.)

(11) Economic Doubts

The dilemma of economic growth is a central theme of this chapter and we shall return to it shortly. There are, however, many other aspects of the workings of the economic system which are perplexing. It is facile to attribute present economic difficulties of the industrialized and oil-importing countries (as many do) to the recent petroleum crisis and to expect a speedy return to "normality". In fact, the international economic boom had come to a standstill already at the beginning of 1973, several months before the spectacular increases in the price of oil.

In post-second world war years, experience seemed to indicate that if the level of total demand was too high, inflation would ensue and, conversely, low demand would generate unemployment. It is therefore with some bewilderment that economists are witnessing the co-existence of unemployment, inflation and sluggish economic growth. It would appear that the system is no longer reacting to the traditional controls. Thorkil Kristensen* has

*Professor Thorkil Kristensen, *The Nature of the Present International Crisis,* Ulriksdal Lecture Series No. 2, Stockholm 1978.

pointed out that this may be due partly to the relatively new phenomenon of highly organized markets within the capitalist system, which have, to some extent, eliminated the self-regulating capacity of the market system. This structural phenomenon is particularly apparent in large scale industrial firms and is a direct consequence of technological developments which are highly capital intensive and induce the producer to attempt to regulate the market in order to reduce risk. Trade union regulation of the labour market functions in the same direction as do cartels, of which OPEC is the most obvious example. Inflation has also resulted in some countries from wage increases and production costs rising more quickly than manpower productivity.

Much more understanding of present economic trends is necessary before a firm management of the system can be re-established. Beyond this, economic policy seems to have drifted away from social policy and concern with human needs; its thinking has been on a too strictly monetary basis, which has tended to leave people out of account. Perhaps the exploratory research towards a new or modified economic system should seek to return towards some of the concepts and visions of the earlier political economy.

(12) Economic Disparities (see Chapter 4)

Despite the two development decades of the United Nations and the years of aid and technical assistance, the gap between the rich and the poor countries continues to widen. Unless progress can be made towards narrowing the gap and more equitable international arrangements made, which give some hope for the future to the masses of underprivileged people, it will be difficult to establish a world of separate, sovereign nations in interdependent harmony. These issues constitute a particularly sensitive zone within the world *problématique* (see p. 23) and are at the heart of the demand for the establishment of a New International Economic Order. Proposals to this end are still at a quite early stage of generality, have not advanced quickly, nor have they been received with much enthusiasm by the industrialized countries, free market or state economy. Nevertheless, discussions at the plenary sessions of the United Nations General Assembly, unofficial assessments and proposals aimed at greater North/South equity such as the RIO Report of the Club of Rome, have greatly extended basic concern with the problem and appreciation of the need for fundamental reassessment of the present system and its operation. One conclusion which is now implicit in the discussions is that any New Order cannot usefully be restricted to the strictly economic, but will have to be seen in a broad context of a social and political nature which includes science and technology amongst its elements. An interesting illustration of the North/South imbalance is given in Fig. 2.

7. TOWARDS ANOTHER KIND OF GROWTH

Having discussed, in general terms, so many of the contemporary issues and trends, we return to the central theme of growth. So far we have considered only the negative aspects of economic growth in the industrialized countries and its insufficiencies in the Third World countries. The positive aspects are, of course, considerable.

Economic growth has yielded immense harvests. It (and the technology on which it is based) has raised man from subsistence and provided the material basis for decency and happiness in life; its benefits have diffused over a large area of the world. It has eliminated the grosser forms of poverty in many places and demonstrated unequivocally that man is capable of eradicating poverty altogether and that he already has the tools to do so. It has given hope, independence, freedom from want, and opportunity; and with it have come many other advances such as those of medical science

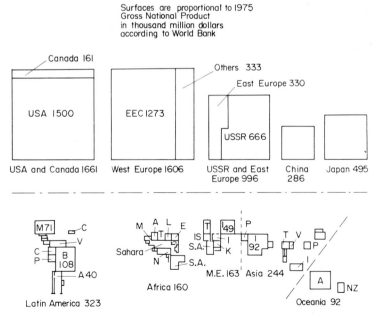

Fig. 2. The 5 powers of the North and the 114 countries of the South. (*Source:* Maurice Guernier, *The Club of Rome.*)

and hygiene that have greatly lowered infant mortality, made possible longer and more vigorous lives, and eliminated many of the age-old diseases of man. The latter benefits have also, of course, contributed greatly to population increase.

It is not surprising, therefore, that continuing high rates of economic growth are still an explicit objective—one of the very few—of nearly all nations, while for the less developed countries, such growth is the primary need, if development is to be achieved. In the industrialized countries there is a growing feeling (still of the minority, it is to be admitted) that the cult of growth with its stress essentially on the material is leading to a leaking away of quality from life; for those near subsistence level, it is probably the only vehicle for increasing life quality.

The fundamental question is, perhaps, the extent to which economic growth contributes to human welfare in the deepest sense. It is certainly essential with regard to providing for the basic human needs such as adequate nutrition, clothing and shelter, health care and education, needs common to all the peoples. But there are human requirements which go far beyond the material necessities and which distinguish the human condition, such as justice and equity, human dignity and the satisfaction of work, a sense of solidarity with the local and national society and of participation in its decisions, the pursuit of self-development and cultural evolution, amongst others. The idea of growth as defined in the Gross National Product changes does not adequately relate to these broader requirements of the good life. The cult of the "more" does not equate with the "better" and tends to neglect the individual with his instinct for quality.

The troubles inherent in the continuation of high rates of growth, some of which are summarized below, are manifold.

(1) One of the most obvious is that growth and its indicator, the Gross National Product (GNP), do not distinguish between productive and socially useful growth and that which is unproductive and even disfunctional. For example, military costs, which in 1978 amounted to a global total of more than $400,000,000,000 and which included of course a considerable "overkill" capacity as well as national prestige and internally repressive elements, can hardly be argued to be productive in the socio-economic sense. Yet they were calmly included by the economists within GNP, whose swollen amount was discussed by politicians and the media in evaluating the prosperity of the nations. Road accidents, drug abuse and hi-jackings contribute to GNP, while home food production, the work of housewives and home improvements by the occupiers are ignored. Destruction of the environment is not subtracted from the index.

(2) Growth encourages environmental damage through pollution from agricultural, industrial and nuclear wastes, by the accumulation of solid waste in the great cities and in many other ways.

(3) Growth demands for its accomplishment increasing quantities of materials and energy at a rate which it may not be possible to sustain indefinitely.

(4) The benefits of growth, as we have seen, are not fairly distributed. In the developing countries, for example, overall growth as measured by GNP was considerable and sustained, while at the same time, the numbers of the poor and hungry increased. This is not inherently the fault of the growth

process as such, but rather the lack of complementary policies of both social and economic nature for the distribution of its benefits to those most in need.

(5) The very success of growth has increased the scale and complexity of human activity and, in the process, greatly magnified the difficulties of governance, leading to the present situation of chronic crisis.

(6) Regular increases over the decades, of a growth based on technological development, have led to it becoming the mainspring of the economic system as such, to the extent that its continuation is essential to the maintenance of society as we know it. The end of growth, especially if sudden, could easily lead to grave social difficulties, massive unemployment and general discontent. Hence the never-ending struggle to expand, to find new markets and create new demands, with a consequent compounding of the difficulties mentioned above.

Thus no-growth policies are quite unlikely to find popular favour. Expectations in the industrialized world, engendered by long years of gradually increasing prosperity, demand the indefinite continuation of material prosperity and social services and this makes it exceedingly difficult for governments to change their policies in face of the massive problems which would be involved. Furthermore there are still many unmet and real social needs even in the richest of countries, while leaders and planners in the Third World are naturally angered by suggestions of zero-growth desirability or the notion that energy and minerals may begin to run out before they are in a position to grasp their fair share. Certainly further growth is necessary, especially for the Third World, but grave problems lie ahead with regard to the adjustment of world patterns of growth and it is highly probable that the presently prosperous countries will be forced by political, economic and moral reasons to modify their consumption demands and expectations. Growth is desirable—yes, but it will have to be another kind of growth.

8. THE NEW INTERNATIONAL ECONOMIC ORDER—ILLUSION OR NECESSITY?

The problems of economic growth are thus to be viewed not in terms of black and white, but within the dimensions of quality—a quality which will vary from culture to culture and which should be defined by each culture. In the past, growth has served society well and made possible the prosperity presently enjoyed by a considerable minority of the world's inhabitants. The Gross World Product has increased by some 250% during the last two decades. Continuation at this rate for a further century would mean another 50-fold increase. Certainly material, energy and environmental constraints would not permit such exponential growth to continue indefinitely, quite apart from the many problems of governance and social management which would emerge. Thus the Limits to Growth are real—the uncertainty is in determining how far ahead they lie and which are the most important. In the meantime, further growth is a necessity for the Third World where basic human needs are far from being met, even at present levels of population. Experience of recent years suggests, however, that new patterns of wealth and growth-distribution are unlikely to be achieved without a considerable modification of the world system, in both the economic and social sense.

The situation is well summarized by Harland Cleveland, writing in one of the background papers for the important study by the Aspen Institute for Humanistic Studies on "the Planetary Bargain". He writes:

There is well-nigh universal agreement on the need for change, and soon. The poorest nations, developing economies without surpluses of oil, food, or major mineral resources, are persuaded by experience that aid-as-charity is not the road to greater social justice or balanced development. Those with valuable raw materials but weak development programs are investing more of their profits in the markets of the rich than the developments of the poor. The developed nations which are poor in resources but rich in industrial and post-industrial skills find themselves embarrassingly dependent on others for oil, food, foreign-exchange and security. And the really rich, efficient in producing food and energy, but wasteful in their use of resources, face unemployment, social tensions and threats to democracy as the outcomes of industrial success.

The need then for some sort of New International Economic Order is manifest. It would have to be based on the realities of interdependence between all the nations of the world, each with its particular needs and contributions and the desirability of achieving a high degree of self-reliance, but not necessarily self-sufficiency in each.

Indeed, the new order could not be restricted to the immediately economic, important though that certainly is. In recent years, decisions have been too much dominated by economic considerations to the exclusion of other values, giving substance to the fears of Burke, that the running of the world might fall into the hands of "economists and sophists". The New Order must aim resolutely at duality as well as equity. The seventh special Session of the Geneva Assembly of the United Nations accepted unanimously a fine statement of desiderata, but there were so many caveats from the developed countries and so much lack of real commitment, that little flesh has yet been put onto the bones of the New Order.

The creation of a New International Economic Order cannot, of course, arise like Venus from the sea, fully shaped, if not fully dressed, by a decision taken by the General Assembly of the United Nations. It will be a matter of long transition from the present order of things towards a more equitable system. Great and sustained efforts and understanding will be demanded from both the industrialized and the developing countries and it would be an illusion on the part of the latter to believe that they can get it here and now simply by gifts from the developed countries or as a result of political pressure. Industrialization of the Third World will be necessary, but not necessarily along the lines already established by the developed nations. Technology transfer, as we shall see later, is not enough. It will be for each nation to establish and evolve technologies appropriate to its cultural, social, economic and environmental needs. In particular, the poor countries will have to go through a long and painful process of internal change within their own societies before they are able to employ the capital and technology which they require and are able to distribute its fruits more fairly to their citizens as a whole.

From the industrialized nations restraint and sacrifice may well be demanded—and above all understanding. If a new order is to succeed it will necessitate a sharing of markets and a geographic redistribution of production facilities. It will entail initial hardships and unpopular decisions, but, if wisely planned, there will be long-term benefits of stability and political harmony. Will the industrialized world have the courage to cooperate in the initiation of this process of restructuring the planetary system? IFIAS is presently carrying out a study on how the transnational corporations might best contribute to the establishing of a basis in developing countries on which they themselves can build a sustained effort of scientific, technological and economic development.

CHAPTER **3**

Areas of Interdependence

Our present situation is marked by a gradual recognition of a whole series of areas of interdependence—between the nations, between the problems they face in common and between the disciplines of learning. It is necessary here to indicate some of the main features of these interdependencies, since they are basic to the comprehension of the emerging situation and suggest the need for a global approach and return to a holistic view of the world.

INTERDEPENDENCE OF THE NATIONS

In a planet of limited dimensions such as ours, with great heterogeneity in the distribution of both energy and mineral resources, of climatic and soil conditions and of regions propitious to a flourishing agriculture and the growth of large human populations, the interdependence of the individual regions and constituent countries is an inevitable phenomenon. Such interdependence between human societies has, of course, always existed, but has not until recently threatened the autonomy or sovereignty of each. In today's world of complexity, however, built as it is on a technology derived from scientific discovery and demanding large and increasing quantities of material and energy resources, by no means always available from local sources, all the countries of the world, with the partial exception of the two superpowers are acting in a situation of mutual dependence which amounts to a *de facto,* but seldom admitted leakage of sovereignty. The extent to which this trend has already advanced is seldom appreciated, moreover it is apparently contradicted by a rampant growth of nationalism and mini-nationalism.

In the past, interdependence has been manifested mainly through international trade and in political and military alliances. In matters of power politics and military might, conquest and threat of conquest, alliances for defence or for military adventure, population pressures and economic forces have always operated, moving over the centuries from the tribal to the city states and from these to the national level and finally to the emerging global situation of today. Technological developments have played a leading role in this transformation, from the replacement of the long bow by the crossbow and the discovery of the military use of gunpowder. Today, nuclear weapons, intercontinental missiles, electronic and other devices for guiding and detecting, and the whole gamut of military hardware and software have become a dominant force in today's foreign policy and the balance of power.

19

In the past, too, military and political relationships have often been closely associated with religious ideology; the forces of Islam and Christendom, for example, have often dominated politics and have forged alliances which have transcended the communality of race or of national self-interest. Such forces are still operative.

International trade is, however, the traditional basis of interdependence and, since many of the essential raw material and energy resources demanded in ever increasing amounts by the industrialized countries lie in distant and often less developed parts of the world, even the strongest of countries are to some extent dependent on the weaker countries. This need, triggered off by the industrial revolution, undoubtedly stimulated the colonial conquests of the last century and is now seen as exploitation.

Economic opportunity ignores national frontiers. The industrial revolution led to the establishment of manufacture close to deposits of coal and iron ore and to the building of great cities on the estuaries of rivers from which industrial products could be distributed throughout the world. This phase is, however, long since past and new industries tend to arise, not in proximity to deposits of minerals and fossil fuels, or even on the traditional manufacturing sites, but near to centres of scientific, technological and managerial skills, on the assumption that reasonably cheap raw materials and energy could always be imported. Japan is a case in point. This country, which has one of the most vigorous economies of the world, has achieved a very high and competitive level of advanced industry, despite its almost complete lack of raw materials and energy, and based on technical skills, forceful policies, growth of research, and high levels of general education. Such dependence on external sources of supply has hitherto been accepted as the normal situation, governed essentially by the forces of the world market. Since the petroleum crisis, however, with its demonstra-

tion of how precarious distant sources of supply may become, and with recognition that the exponential growth of demand may lead to scarcity and high prices of the basic commodities, such dependence must be looked at in a new way. This has become, indeed, one of the facets of interdependence, implicitly accepted as one of the bargaining points of the developing countries in pressing for a New International Economic Order.

There are, of course, many other instances of interdependence. The monetary system, with its uncertain controls is a constant irritant today. Again, the contagion of rampant inflation in so many countries simultaneously is no coincidence and appears to be outside the control of individual governments. Even violence, encouraged at times by a deep sense of injustice and at others by an insane fanaticism, has become internationalized and made greatly more effective as a result of the availability and ease of manufacture of weapons and other technical devices as well as by the vulnerability of technological installations, aircraft, etc.

What is new in the situation of interdependence is that it has reached a new level of magnitude at which it is beginning to restrict the power of the individual governments to control fully, their own national destinies. The new elements, we have already marked; they are the vastly increased level of human activity and of international transactions, the rapid rate of change, and a generalization of expectations on a world scale. As Stanley Hoffman, the political scientist, puts it, "the vessel of sovereignty is leaking". Yet the concept of the nation state is apparently unassailable; it corresponds well to the interests of those who possess power, while for many of the recently independent, developing countries whose populations consist of a somewhat artificial mix of tribes, brought together as a consequence of lines drawn on the map by rival, colonial powers a century or more ago, a fragile sovereignty is one of the few elements of cohesion and must be maintained at all costs. We are not likely, therefore, to see a replacement of the present system of nation states by a world government in the foreseeable future, but rather a *de facto* erosion of elements of sovereignty by consent, through an increasing amount of international consultation, regulation, and cooperative ventures as the global problems of concern to all countries become more pressing. But an international mechanism to meet such needs effectively will have to be very different from those of today.

The classification of the planet into the traditional three worlds of the market economies, the state economies and the developing countries has proved useful for political and other purposes, but even if one adds the Fourth World, as is now common, of the oil producing countries, rich, but in many ways still underdeveloped, the traditional classification is quite insufficient for our present purposes. The Third World represents, in fact, a whole spectrum of development levels, potential riches, environments, cultural determinants and the like, while in the First World, prospects for the future are very diverse from instances of great riches in the form of natural resources, to extreme poverty in these. We therefore propose a more dynamic model of four worlds as indicated in Fig. 3, with the possibility of some countries crossing the classification lines as a result of probable developments.

In Fig. 3, the horizontal axis shows potential resource capacity rising from right to left, while the vertical axis indicates level of economic development rising from the bottom to the top. Thus the top, left-hand quadrant contains countries rich in resources and in existing economic achievement, that at the top, right-hand side, nations, already highly developed economically but short of natural resources. The bottom left-hand quadrant groups the countries at a lower level of economic development but potentially rich in consequence of their resource possession, while the fourth (bottom, right) consists of these nations at low prosperity and resource levels. A few countries are marked on the diagram to indicate the general spread in the system, but no attempt has been made to estimate quantitative accuracy. The weakness of this method of classification is that it is unable to distinguish between general and economic development, hence, for example, the position of the OPEC countries is somewhat ambiguous. It does, however, give a good indication of the potentiality for future transitions and the nature of the dependencies and hints at how different will be the research priorities and policies of each category.

Despite the wide differences between the countries of the Third World, which we have stressed, many feel that the concept has its uses in grouping together those countries which have an excessive dependence on others. We doubt the validity of this in view of the interdependence of *all* countries.

THE INTERDEPENDENCE OF PROBLEMS AND POLICIES

We have already listed some of the contemporary problems which are faced by the world as a whole. The interaction or interdependence of these and other problems is quickly obvious and it follows that such interactions must have serious consequences for the policy areas concerning each. In fact, interdependence of problems connotes interdependence of the different areas of policy. This, in turn, raises difficult questions concerning the ability of the machinery of government to cope with the interactions, a subject which we shall discuss at length later.

Let us mention a few of the more obvious interactions between a few of the main problem areas. Energy production, increased use of materials and even agricultural intensification have a marked impact on the environment which if sufficiently modified could, through climatic change, inhibit agricultural yields.

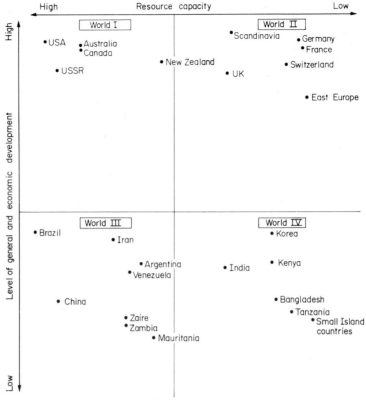

Fig. 3.

Demographic structures and trends can affect employment, incommensurate with the total population increase in some Third World countries, while in the First World, through increase in the average age of the population, they influence educational planning on the one hand and can throw great burdens on the health and welfare services.

The energy situation illustrates well the complexities and the difficulties faced by the traditional governmental structure in coping with them. The recent petroleum crisis demonstrated how widely diffused the energy problem is, how solutions involve both short and long term considerations and have implications for, and repercussions on, practically all sectors of the economy and society. The political issues concerned with securing adequate supplies of oil,

focussed initially on the Arab-Israeli question, but they soon raised much wider political questions, such as the policy of Japan towards the Soviet Union and China, the coherence of the European Common Market, the aid policies of the United States and the situation of the Third World countries for which the raising of petroleum prices was a particular hardship, especially in relation to the energy-intensive manufacture of fertilizers needed for the production of more food for bigger populations. The economic consequences have been profound through deterioration of the balance of payments of the oil-importing countries, aggravation of inflation and the distortion of the investment pattern. Scientific and technological policies were affected in view of the need to develop substitutes for petroleum, through a wide spread of options including reversion to, and increase of, coal production (with all the social and technical problems which this entails), nuclear fission and fusion (bringing again a whole series of social, technical and economic issues), solar energy capture, etc. Environmental and social consequences are obvious; while there is still a considerable social resistance to the erection of new power stations, pipelines and oil refineries, the material discomforts of energy shortage and high costs greatly weakened the environmental lobby, at least for the moment. In the United States, resistance to the Alaska pipeline melted away and rigid legislation for the catalytic cleaning of automobile exhaust fumes was delayed when it was realized that such measures entailed increased fuel consumption.

The contemporary problems exist, therefore, as an untidy tangle of intertwining difficulties which is now often referred to as the "world *problématique*". Nearly all of them are the direct or indirect consequences of technological development or have important scientific facets. We are facing, not a series of discrete difficulties which can be clearly delineated and tackled successfully one by one, but a cluster of interacting problems so tangled the one with the others, that it is increasingly difficult to formulate discrete problems and apply discrete solutions, without disturbing other, and often apparently remote, areas of the tangle. To attempt to solve individual strands of the *problématique* in isolation seems, therefore, like removing the external symptoms of a disease which has not been fully diagnosed. Removal of symptoms may initially appear to be an improvement or even a cure, but it can often change the balance of the system as a whole and give rise to the breaking out of other symptoms elsewhere in the body, not immediately recognisable as connected to the original difficulty. The confused tangle of the *problématique* is illustrated through a few of its identifiable interconnections in Fig. 4.

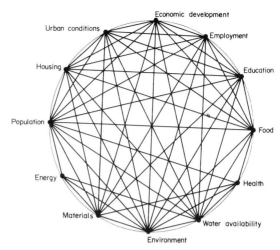

Fig. 4. The tangle of the *problématique*.

To be more faithful to reality the lines of the diagram should not be straight, but rather tangled, spiralling fibrils. Within the *problématique,* each zone is itself complex, with economic, social, political and technological elements which require attack through a transdisciplinary approach. The *problématique* thus becomes a political as well as an intellectual reality.

THE INTERDEPENDENCE OF THE SCIENTIFIC DISCIPLINES

The third area of interdependence with which we are concerned relates to science itself. The fundamental changes now taking place in the operation of the world system and the need to understand the deeper interactions of the *problématique* will have an influence on the nature of intellectual activity and on the research and educational structures. An immediate necessity, as we have seen, is for multidisciplinary attack on many of the contemporary problems. Although a great deal of lip service is paid to this idea, very little is in fact done about it. The structures of the universities and the research institutes is still mainly monodisciplinary— equally "vertical" as the sectoral arrangements of governments. Certainly, deep specialization in research is as essential as ever in uncovering new knowledge, but in addition there is a need to complement this by a new generation of scientists, deeply versed in their original discipline, but capable and willing to cooperate with others from different subjects, to communicate with them and help to provide new insights and new solutions in attacking the problems of society. The present career structure and merit systems of *academia* work to prevent just this. Promotion depends essentially on the judgement of peers in a narrowly specialized field, based on published work. A man who has collaborated with scientists of other disciplines, perhaps brilliantly in a multidisciplinary team, is often regarded as something of a dilettante and passed over in promotion. This is perhaps a temporary phenomenon since there is already a demonstrated need for broadly-based individuals, deeply versed in a particular discipline, but willing and able to work and communicate with those in other fields as members of a composite team. Career prospects should thus arise within this transdisciplinary perspective.

There are, however, much deeper forces operating within scientific development itself, which indicates a further independence between the various scientific subjects. From its origin, during the Renaissance, experimental science, or natural philosophy as it was then called was regarded in a holistic and universalist sense. *La Science, Wissenschaft, Nauk,* and the corresponding term in many other languages was regarded as equivalent to systematic knowledge, although approached with a new and experimental orientation. The individuals who founded the Royal Society of London in the middle of the seventeenth century, for example, included clerics, generalists and intellectuals in many fields, in addition to the new breed of experimental scientists. It was only late in the nineteenth century that the Anglo-Saxon heresy began to regard science in terms of the quickly-growing experimental subjects such as chemistry, physics and biology and excluding the social and humanistic disciplines. This tendency soon began to become generalized, as a consequence of the great advances in the natural sciences and the increasing extent of their specialization. Thus the national science policies of many countries today are generally conceived in terms of the natural sciences and engineering. Although there is a new concern with the social sciences, or at least a realization that the social aspects of problems must be considered at the same time as the technical aspect, their resource support is often marginal.

The exigencies of the times demand a reversal of this, not only by the inclusion of the social sciences in national policies, but in devising a more dynamic and flexible approach to intellectual activity as a whole. In the universities and elsewhere, science is still taught and practised in terms of the classification of the sciences devised in the middle of the nineteenth century—a series of neat little compartments labelled chemistry, physics, botany, geology, etc. As the content of these sciences built up, interface sciences such as biochemistry or chemical physics began to emerge and had to be accepted as separate entities, while later more complicated intersections such as molecular biology, or cybernetics. More recently still, less clearly defined topics of growth began to emerge, which depended on inputs from more than two sciences. Such a topic is that of brain and behaviour which lies at the intersection of a number of disciplines including molecular biology, neurophysiology, biochemistry, anthropology, and psychiatry; its progress depends on the intellectual contributions from research in these and other fields, very difficult to assembly together, with present structures and attitudes. Such subjects are, in fact, not permanent disciplines of new categories of science, but temporary subjects, foci of scientific advance across the frontiers of knowledge, which can be consolidated only through multidisciplinary attack. They will usually extend later by merger with other, equally transient, footholds of knowledge to form still newer, and probably equally temporary, outposts on the borders of understanding, within which, the appropriate regiments of science will muster, for still further penetration into the unknown.

Such may indeed be the general pattern of scientific development of the future, not only individual disciplines extending, as it were, linearly, but also a dynamic interaction of various lines of approach from different subjects within the total fabric of knowledge, advancing where and when promising openings appear or where complex problems lead. Inevitably such an approach must encompass the social and behavioural sciences and eventually also the humanities. This would indeed be a return to the universal concept of Science.

This dynamic concept of the evolution of the scientific system corresponds to the other interdependencies we have described. It fits ill with the present intellectual structures and attitudes, just as do the other interdependencies with the political and administrative counterparts. There is indeed great need for institutional experiment and innovation.

CHAPTER **4**

The Resource Base—
the Carrying Capacity of
the Planet

The opinion we have expressed that the real limits to man's achievements are political and social, does not exclude the reality of the physical difficulties of providing the resources for the solution, or amelioration, of the complex problems which we have outlined. The assumption of unlimited and cheap resources has been the basis of the growth phenomenon and hence of hopes for the social design of the future. Any uncomfortable views to the contrary have been rejected as Malthusian and hence discredited by the intellectuals and brushed aside by the political leaders as rocking the boat and necessitating rethinking of virtually all the social assumptions on which contemporary public policy is based. Now, however, we have discovered that the apparently limitless blue sky of the future has a ceiling and that it is just possible that we are within reach of it. Given adequate resources, and especially plentiful and cheap energy, research and, above all, time, it might be possible to raise the ceiling significantly. The greatest doubt is as to whether we have the time. Three potential ma-

jor bottlenecks have to be examined if we are to avoid crisis in the near future. These are:

—adequacy of capital availability;

—production and distribution of food;

—the extent to which resources such as land, water, energy and minerals can be extended.

1. CAPITAL FLOWS AND AVAILABILITY

Provision of the infrastructure to provide the necessities for a very much bigger population and to operate the world system on the increased scale will demand enormous capital resources in a short time. For example, replacement of petroleum, which will in any case become scarce and costly within a few decades, by non-traditional forms of energy such as fusion, solar or geothermal, or even by extension of nuclear fission reactors, will necessitate an unthinkable high annual capital provision. It may in fact be necessary to rebuild the greater part of the world system for production and use of energy in a few decades—at an enormous capital cost.

Areas where demand for capital is likely to increase in the future, in addition to energy and mineral resources development, include environment and conservation, health, transportation, education, water resources, housing and new technological development.

Capital is created essentially by human effort and by saving a significant proportion of the fruits of production. A society which consumes most of what it produces cannot expect to accumulate sufficient capital for development. The ratios of saving to GNP differ much from country to country. They are high in Japan at about 30% and in West Germany at about 25%, but below 15% in most of the developing countries. Investment demand is variable according to economic conditions. Consequently, there may be cases where capital appears in excess supply as it did in advanced industrial countries under the worldwide depression of 1975. It does not imply, however, that there is no need for increasing savings in a global context and in the longer run.

The impacts of oil price change and economic slump within the advanced countries on the non-oil-exporting less developed countries (LDCs) were traumatic. In 1975 their average growth rates were almost cut in half from the relatively favourable rates of about 6% experienced in the early 1970s. To accomplish even that reduced-growth performance, heavy reliance on external financing in the private capital markets of the advanced countries and increased official aid flows were needed. The net transfer of financial resources to non-oil-exporting LDCs almost doubled between 1971-3 and 1974-6 (from approximately $20 billion annually to over $37 billion annually).* Forty per cent of the net flow of financial

*The Global Economic Challenge, Vol. I. Trade, Commodities, Capital Flows. The United Nations Association of the USA. New York, 1978.

resources to LDCs in 1974-6 represented increased credits from Western commercial banks. Concern over the indebtedness of LDCs to commercial banks and the capacity of borrowers to service and ultimately repay that debt was an inevitable result of the massive changes in external financial flows since 1974.

It is convenient to separate international problems according to their dimensions of time. These relate to financing for short-term balance-of-payments shortfalls, for intermediate-term financing of balance-of-payments adjustment, and for long-term financing of economic development.

Short-term balance-of-payments financing refers to foreign exchange requirements to maintain essential inputs while avoiding substantial currency depreciations of severe control measures when a balance-of-payments disturbance is unexpected and temporary. Such legitimate financing needs, for example, may arise from national disasters, crop failures or temporary declines in export earnings.

Intermediate-term financial requirements arise when a substantial permanent shock to a country's balance-of-payments occurs. It is frequently advantageous—and sometimes essential to stretch out the process of economic adjustment to the new equilibrium over several years, requiring that the balance-of-payments deficits in the intervening years be financed by a decline in the nation's international resources or an increase in its external liabilities, i.e. in its external debt.

The oil-price changes of 1973-4 were a dramatic shock, raising greatly the intermediate balance-of-payments financing needs of oil-importing countries.

Unlike short- and intermediate-term balance-of-payments financing, longer term development financing is normally for sizable projects and for national development institutions that generate additional capital formation in the borrowing country.

Short- and intermediate-financing needs are most often associated with balance-of-payments disturbances and adjustments, while sources of funds for long-term financing can be thought of as contributing to capital formation and growth in the borrowing economy.

To achieve the transition to a more stable world financial system, basic changes in policies and institutions must take place. However, the full range of economic development and adjustment policies cannot be dealt with by changes in financial policies and institutions alone. Fundamentally important are policies in the advanced countries and in the LDCs relating the economic growth, international trade, international investment and concessionary development assistance.

A healthy and viable international financial mechanism is of direct interest to both the LDCs and the advanced countries and is a requisite for a dynamic and growing independent world economy.

Interdependence of economies is now at its highest point in history. Economic performance in the advanced countries is partly dependent upon economic growth and economic policies in the LDCs, and vice versa. Economic disturbances are transmitted quickly through the international economic system, and an elastic financial network is needed which can absorb and spread shocks over larger periods of time, so as to allow extended adjustment to the mutual economic advantage of non-oil-developing countries, oil producers and the industrial countries.

An allocation of international investment in an effective and efficient manner is necessary to develop new resources and markets, create jobs for the many millions entering the labour force, and avoid retrenchments into protectionist and inward-looking economic policies. A financial network is required which is not disrupted or threatened by normal and expected shocks to the international economy from cyclical, technological or policy changes.

The best assurance of a sound financial structure is one in which the economic and financial performances of borrowers—both public and private—provide the ability to repay. In an interdependent world, this also means that disturbances in the international economy are not allowed to compromise quickly that repayment capacity. In short, a margin for contingencies is needed in the international financial system.

There is at present, a (presumably temporary) trend towards reduction rather than increase in the global demand for capital. This is, to a large extent, a result of the transfer of a substantial part of the world annual surplus to the oil exporting countries which can by no means fully absorb it. Slower economic growth in the industrialized countries, which now seems likely, will also work in this direction. A main cause of the present high levels of unemployment in these countries is a sharp increase in the savings of households, but this does not help the poor countries who, fortunately, are now receiving more aid from the oil producers. In the longer perspective, however, global demand for capital for purposes such as we have outlined is highly probable.

As regards capital formation, there are many problems such as how the ratio of savings which constitute its sources could be raised, or how investment could be directed to sectors where such investment is really needed, or how productivity of capital could be increased.

Increases in the savings ratio will require prevention of wasteful spendings by governments and individuals, which will in turn necessitate new life-styles. Reductions in defence expenditures by various countries would be an important means to increase savings. There is also need to transfer savings in the developed countries to capital-deficient developing countries through aid or long-term investment. It will be essential for the growth of the world as a whole that foreign exchanges accumulated by oil-producing countries are used in assisting development in non-oil-producing developing countries. Institutions and development banks are now being formed in several of the oil-producing countries for recycling of the gigantic oil export surplus capital to development programmes in LDCs. Developing countries, on their part, will be required not to waste but to use effectively the aid and investment they have received.

The situation becomes more grave in the oil-importing nations, combining both capital and energy shortages they could be so hard pressed by unemployment, inflation, lowering of living standards, social tensions and the threat of societal collapse, that they might be tempted in desperation to impose totalitarian solutions or even to resolve the crisis by military force.

At the same time the developing countries, faced with population increase, capital shortage and hunger, would attempt to break out of their difficulties by mass emigration to unsaturated territories with consequent strife and calamity.

These may be extreme consequences but not unthinkable and we can only hope to avoid such difficulties by taking early action. The Mesarovič—Pestel report* to the Club of Rome indicates clearly how, without final disaster, the cost of delay in taking decisions on many critical matters involves monstrous costs in money, material resources and human suffering. (See Figs. 5 and 6.)

2. THE PRODUCTION AND DISTRIBUTION OF FOOD

The production of adequate nourishment is the primary basis of individual survival. There is in fact enough food in the world today to

*E. Pestel and M. Mesarovič, *Mankind at the Turning Point,* 2nd Report to the Club of Rome.

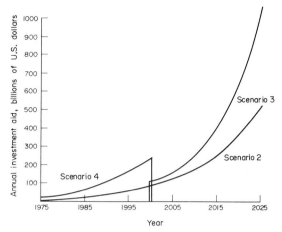

In each of the three scenarios considered here, the aid is given with the purpose of cutting the *per capita* income ratio between the above-named developing regions and the developed world (Regions 1-4) to 1 to 3 for Latin America and 5 to 1 for South Asia and Tropical Africa. In Scenario 2 aid is given continuously for 50 years, in Scenario 3 the beginning aid is delayed until the year 2000, while in Scenario 4 aid is given only during the last quarter of this century. The enormous advantage of giving aid on a large scale as early as possible (Scenario 4) is only too obvious.

Fig. 5. Total annual investment aid provided by the developed world to Latin America, South Asia and Tropical Africa. (From E. Pestel and M. Mesarovič, *Mankind at the Turning Point,* 2nd Report to the Club of Rome.)

feed everyone, if the current production were equitably distributed, which it is not. Fig. 7 shows that there was indeed sufficient supply to cover the requirement in 1972-4. Table 4 gives the absolute numbers of persons below the critical limit. In the industrialized countries agricultural productivity is high and can be increased, although at a high cost, while population growth (less than 1%) is low. In the less developed countries, on the contrary, agricultural yields and productivity are very low, population increase is more than 2% and in places more than 3.5% per annum. It is therefore in the developing countries that a dramatic push is needed to increase food-growing productivity, but we cannot expect early success.

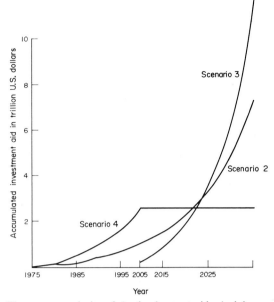

The great superiority of the development aid schedule according to Scenario 4 is impressive. It shows how important and, at the same time, cost saving it is to help the developing countries as quickly as possible to gain their economic take-off point. The cost of aid as measured by the accumulated investment in the case of early action is less than one fourth the cost in the case of delayed action.

Fig. 6. Accumulated investment aid (1975-2025). (From E. Pestel and M. Mesarovič, *Mankind at the Turning Point,* 2nd Report to the Club of Rome.)

For the future there are two schools whose views at first sight appear contradictory. The pessimists hold that there is a desperate race between increasing numbers of hungry mouths and relatively decreasing supplies, while the optimists protest that there is a capacity to feed many times the population of the world. There is indeed much truth in both approaches. The fact that there is starvation and widespread undernutrition today, while food supplies are still ample, demonstrates clearly that the difficulties so far have been essentially those of distribution economics and the political system. Food is costly to produce; the hungry are poor and unable to buy it! This present situation augurs badly for the future, when the total population will have doubled and indicates the urgency of *preparing now,* both at the political, economic, logistic and technical levels, for a situation which will inevitably develop.

The basically political nature of this problem, however, does not excuse us from examining the extent to which and whether the limitations of land, water, energy, fertilizers, scientific knowledge and other factors do really allow of indefinite expansion without causing major disturbances throughout the *problématique* which would in the end boomerang to prevent the necessary expansion of food supplies.

The present world production of food is about 1,200 million tons of cereals per annum which, if evenly distributed, would allow of 330 kg per annum *per capita;* the survival level is estimated to be around 200 kg *per capita.* Against this, the average annual growth has been about 30 million tons of which a bit over 70% has, until recently, been absorbed by population increase, the rest contributing to increased supplies or quality, mainly in support of affluence. It should be realized, however, that while in the LDCs, most of the grain is consumed directly by human beings, in the industrialized countries there is only a small proportional intake of cereals and a high meat protein demand. In Canada, for example, just over 10% of the grain *per capita* is consumed directly, the rest of the carbohydrate being converted to protein through the inefficient medium of livestock, while in India, in contrast, direct consumption of the grain *per capita* amounts to about 83%. In LDCs, as development proceeds, there is a tendency for people, especially in the more privileged classes, to increase their meat protein demands likewise. If the world as a whole were to achieve by the year 2000 the present western European dietary level of 500 kg *per capita,* the total production would have to increase 250% to some 3,000 million tons. A United States diet for everybody would entail a 400% increase of food production.

Per caput calorie supply and requirement in 1972-74

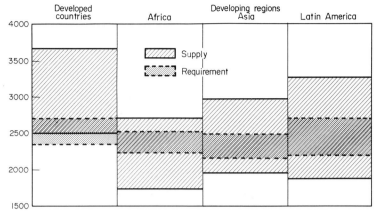

Fig. 7. *Per caput* calorie supply and requirement in 1972-4. *(Source: The Fourth
World Food Survey,* FAO 1977)

TABLE 4

*Estimated Number of Persons with Food Intake Below the Critical Minimum Limit:
Developing Regions (Excluding Asian Centrally Planned Economies)**

Region	Total population (Millions)		Percentage below 1.2 BMR		Total number below 1.2 BMR (Millions)		
	1969-71	1972-4	1969-71	1972-4	1969-71	1972-4	(revised)
Africa	278	301	25	28	70	83	
Far East	968	1,042	25	29	256	297	
Latin America	279	302	16	15	44	46	
Near East	167	182	18	16	31	20	
MSA†	954	1,027	27	30	255	307	
Non-MSA	738	800	20	18	146	148	
Developing countries	1,692	1,827	24	25	401	455	

*The difference between figures given in this table for 1969-71 differs from those quoted in the document
Assessment of the world food situation, present and future, presented at the World Food Conference
1974, largely due to revisions in the estimates of *per caput* food supplies as well as in the population
figures.
†MSA: most seriously affected.
Source: The Fourth World Food Survey, FAO 1977.

The recent history of expansion of food production has been impressive; between 1950 and
1970 cereal growth has doubled while population increased only 50%. However, distribution
has been very uneven owing to the tendency of
the rich countries to demand ever increasing
proportion of protein, to the extent that the
health consequences are disturbing.* According
to World Watch Institute, "over the last decade

**The Two Faces of Malnutrition,* Eric Eckholm, World
Watch Institute, Report No. 9.

TABLE 5

Rates of Growth of Agricultural Production in Relation to Population:
World and Regions, 1961-5 to 1970 and 1970-6

Region	Total population		Agricultural production			
			Total		Per caput	
	1961-5 to 1970	1970-6	1961-5 to 1970	1970-6	1961-5 to 1970	1970-6
Developed market economies	1.0	0.9	1.9	2.2	0.9	1.3
North America	1.2	0.9	1.4	2.8	0.2	1.9
Western Europe	0.7	0.6	2.2	1.6	1.5	1.0
Oceania	1.8	1.7	2.8	1.3	1.0	-0.4
Other developed market economies	1.4	1.6	3.1	2.0	1.7	0.4
Eastern Europe and the USSR	1.0	0.9	2.8	2.0	1.8	1.1
All developed countries	1.0	0.9	2.2	2.1	1.2	1.2
Developing market economies	2.6	2.6	3.1	2.6	0.5	0.0
MSA countries	2.4	2.5	3.1	1.9	0.6	-0.5
Non-MSA countries	2.7	2.7	3.1	3.1	0.4	0.4
Africa	2.5	2.7	2.7	1.1	0.2	-1.5
Latin America	2.7	2.8	2.9	2.9	0.2	0.1
Near East	2.7	2.8	3.1	3.9	0.4	1.1
Far East	2.5	2.5	3.3	2.6	0.8	0.1
Other developing market economies	2.5	2.5	2.3	1.6	-0.2	-0.8
Asian centrally planned economies	1.8	1.7	2.8	2.5	1.0	0.7
All developing countries	2.3	2.3	3.0	2.5	0.7	0.2
World	1.9	1.9	2.5	2.3	0.6	0.4

Source: *The Fourth World Food Survey,* FAO 1977.

food production in both the developed and developing countries has expanded about 30%. This expansion has resulted in a substantial (15%) increase in the *per capita* food production in the developed countries.'' The Green Revolution has undoubtedly helped greatly in this; it has bought time for us. Although it has had some disturbing side effects, it is doubtful if it can now enable us to keep ahead of population increase. In Table 5 and Fig. 8 are presented the food production and the rates of growth in relation to the population for different regions of the world.

According to FAO the future necessary increase of food production is 3.6% per annum. A likely level in practice is about 3% per annum over the next 40 to 50 years, but many feel that even this growth rate may prove too optimistic. According to FAO again, the deficit by 1985 is likely to be 76 millions tons per year and this is estimated to rise later to around 100 million tons per annum, which is a threat to the sur-

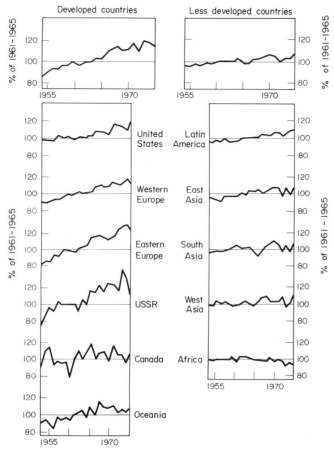

Fig. 8. World food production *per capita,* 1954-1975. The developing countries have gained only 0.4% per year. In none of those regions has the index reached 110, and in Africa it has shown a downward trend since 1951. *Per capita* food production trended upward 1.5% per year in the developed countries until the early 1970s. In each of those regions the index of *per capita* food production has reached or exceeded 110 at least three times in the 22-year period. (Adapted from US Department of Agriculture, *The world food situation and prospects to 1985,* Foreign Agricultural Economic Report No. 98, 1974; recent data from WAS-12.)

vival of about 500 million people. Already today, we know that approximately 570 million people are subject to constant starvation.

Another aspect of this problem is the irregularity and uncertainty of harvest yields. The IFIAS project on the implications of prob-able climatic change indicates that a continuation of the equable climatic conditions of recent decades cannot be assumed, and that we must expect a period of deteriorating weather conditions and extremes which could have an exceedingly deleterious influence on world agricultural production. The year 1972, with the failure of the Russian wheat crop, the irregularity of the monsoons and the continuation of the Sahel drought, may be a more common type of occurrence in the future. This same year saw an actual decline in world food production, while the population rose by a further 70 million. Furthermore, world reserves of food stocks which in 1961 represented 105 days' consumption, had fallen by the end of 1975 to barely one month's needs. This raises the question of building up reserve stocks to a level at which they could provide a real buffer to year by year fluctuations of agricultural yields. The most obvious solution would be the creation of internationally owned and managed buffer stocks, but there is still much opposition to this approach, particularly on economic arguments. The longer we wait, the higher the population level will be, and hence the greater the difficulty in producing reserves. This problem of reserves is therefore a matter of considerable urgency. The low yields of Soviet wheat in 1975, with its consequences of high import demands by that country to maintain its increasing levels of food affluence, makes this difficult at present. It should be noted, however, that recent, remarkably good, harvests in countries such as India, could make the building up of food reserves easier.

For the year 1977, it has been officially reported that the total Soviet crop was reduced from the predicted 220 million tons to about 195 million tons, a reduction by nearly 15%.

IFIAS has just finished its 2½-year study called "Drought and Man: the 1972 Case History". It will be published by Pergamon Press during 1979 in several volumes dealing with both the climatological and socio-political dimensions of drought as a natural catastrophe. A few of the main conclusions may be of interest to mention here.

The more or less accepted version of what happened around 1972, is that, as a result of the fall in world food production caused by climatic anomalies, the Soviet Union and the developing countries purchased large quantities of grain, which led to a depletion of stocks and exceptional price increase of grain and other foodstuffs. This version is questioned by the IFIAS project. In 1972, there was a decrease of 2.2% in the world production of cereals as compared with the previous year. However, the increase in production between 1970 and 1971 was 8.5%; the 1972 production was 5.4% *greater* than in 1970 and was more than the average for five preceding years by 5.7%. The average increase over the three years, 1971-3, including the decrease in 1972, was 54.4 million tons, i.e. more than double the increase indicated by FAO as necessary to compensate for the greater demand for consumption. The IFIAS study concludes that the fluctuations in the international grain trade and, in particular, the price variations, during the period 1972-5, do not reflect a deficit in food production, nor changes in the food requirements of the developing countries. They seem rather to be the result of a changing policy concerning the structure of the world food production and trade and not the accidental effect of climatic phenomena or the inevitable consequence of a gradual increase in demand due to demographic pressure.

In view of the above, it is comforting to find that the "Food Fund" proposed at the UN Food Conference in Rome 1974 , was finally established by the end of 1977. Its primary function is to help Third World countries in situations of food supply emergencies so that they can afford to buy on the world market to meet basic needs of food.

The current situation is, however, still somewhat discouraging for the maintenance of even the 3% increase mentioned above. In Third World countries, where food production has been stagnating or has even declined recently because of high prices and restricted availability of essential imports such as fuel and fertilizers, adequate financial support is necessary to compensate for erosion in the ability to import. Furthermore, the oil-importing Third World countries have had to cut back public investment in real terms as a consequence of global inflation. Consequently, investment in areas such as irrigation, which is essential if food yields are to be increased, has been delayed or abandoned.

The prospects of developing non-agricultural and non-traditional food sources are not too promising in the short term. It is doubtful if much can be obtained quickly from fisheries whose production has been going down, although there may be some eventual additions from the catching of species not yet welcomed as food or of krill in the Antarctic when the whales are no more there to eat them. Likewise, there is no real scientific breakthrough with regard to the cultivation of single cell proteins, hydroponics or synthetic foods on a scale to make much difference.

Very considerable contributions could be made by research to increasing traditional agriculture and in this priority must be given to tropical conditions and crops, including some not yet systematically cultivated. The results of such work, although they will no doubt be significant for the future, even when successful, can have little generalized influence this century, owing to the length of the research process and the biological life cycle.

Special efforts should be devoted to reducing the energy requirements, including fertilizer intake of agriculture. Promising openings begin to appear in the fixation of atmosphere nitrogen, some of which will be sketched here.

Support of terrestrial life depends not only on photosynthesis, which allows the plant to utilize the sun's energy in synthesizing sugars and starch from atmospheric carbon dioxide, but also in the fixation of nitrogen from the air, which is necessary for plant growth and, of course, for the production of protein. As nitrogen in the soil is depleted, agricultural production fails. Replenishment of the nitrogen may be by biological fixation or by the addition of industrially produced fertilizers. The cost, inefficiency, and possible environmental disadvantages, of increased use of chemical fertilizers gives importance to the need to develop new biological fixation methods.

The growing of legume crops, which have nodules of nitrogen-fixing bacteria in their roots, is the traditional method of introducing biological nitrogen through crop rotation systems. It is now realized, however, that a much wider range of micro-organisms, both free-living and in various symbiotic relationships with plants, are capable of fixing nitrogen and this opens the way to explore how these can be manipulated for agricultural use.

One approach is to improve the use and effectiveness of legumes in agriculture, for example by giving importance to the nodulation and nitrogen-fixation systems in breeding, innoculation of legumes, and elimination of limiting factors from production systems. Such approaches seem to have great potential for bringing into agricultural production great areas, at present uncultivated, of tropical savannahs.

In this connection it is interesting to mention recent discoveries of fast growing plants in the tropics which seem to have a great potential both for fodder and fuel production.

Leucaena leucocephala or the "Hawaiian Giant" as it is popularly called is a legumenous plant which grows about 5-6 metres per year without nitrogen fertilizer and with small amounts of water. It can even tolerate saline water. Recent experiments in India* show that the production can be as high as 20 tons per ha. with 25% protein and 30% dry mass for cattle fodder. The stems can be used both as construction material and firewood.

*The Bharatiya Agro-Industries Foundation, Central Campus, Uruli-Kanchan Dist., Poona, India. (Private communication.)

A less traditional possibility arises from recently discovered associations of new nitrogen-fixing bacteria with tropical grasses and some grain crops such as rice, sorghum, millet and maize, which are as yet insufficiently explored and not exploited.

Still more distant prospects are held out by the possibility of genetic engineering in the manipulation of nitrogen fixation elements in various bacteria and plants, resulting from the discovery of mechanisms for transfer of nitrogenase synthesis genes between bacteria, the production of depressant mutants of bacteria able to fix nitrogen even in the presence of ammonia. Possibilities also exist for producing new nitrogen-fixing plants by tissue culture techniques, protoplast fusion techniques—but again we must stress that these are, from a practical point of view, distant prospects.

Considerable advances are possible in the elimination of wastage in agricultural products and stored crops, particularly in the poorer countries. Over-all food losses due to pests such as rats, insects and fungi may amount to 20% or more of the total food supply of the world in any one year, and FAO figures indicate that such pests destroy annually some 33 million tons of food in store, which equals the annual growth. Further invisible losses occur from bad health conditions, again many in the poorer countries, where intestinal worms, infantile diarrhoea, etc., may remove as much as one third of ingested food from human nourishment. Much of these losses could be eliminated by better harvesting procedures, improved storage facilities, better hygiene, etc., but this would involve high capital expenditure, better techniques, etc., which we cannot expect to be forthcoming very soon.

Efforts to achieve the desired 3.6% increase in agricultural yields must rely greatly on the intensification of *existing* agricultural practices, which depend largely on major investment in facilities, modern machinery and other equipment and not least on fertilizer availability.

There are some reasons to hope that new genetic strains, for example of rice, coupled with improved practices, will provide some increase in the near future; but this is unlikely to be sufficient, especially in view of the increased costs of energy, for fertilizers and machinery. There will be need, then, to supplement the agricultural products of the high population-growth areas by import from industrialized, food-producing countries such as Canada, Australia and, above all, the United States, which are capable in theory of making up the world cereal deficit. Agriculture in such countries is highly energy-intensive and therefore much more expensive than in the developing countries. A kilocalorie of food in North America requires for its production several kilocalories of oil, in contrast to the O-K calorie in Indian or African agriculture today. Interesting comparisons of the energy subsidy in different food producing systems have been made by Slesser. The results of typical energy subsidies are presented in Fig. 9. At this level, agriculture becomes not simply the production of carbohydrates through solar-energy by photosynthesis, but essentially the conversion of stored fossil fuel energy to food energy. The consumption of oil would in practice be bearable as would be the economic disruption, if this were attempted on the massive scale which might be required even if one did not raise the question of who will pay for the hundreds of millions of tons which might be required. Distribution again would be overloaded: railway transportation to the ports, long sea hauls, and complicated distribution to the innumerable villages at the receiving end. The transportation of oil, minerals and food already accounts for three-quarters of the world's shipping; to double this capacity is beyond immediate reach.

No, the main effort must be in agricultural intensification in the Third World countries and for a large proportion of the world's area, subsistence farming is likely to continue as in

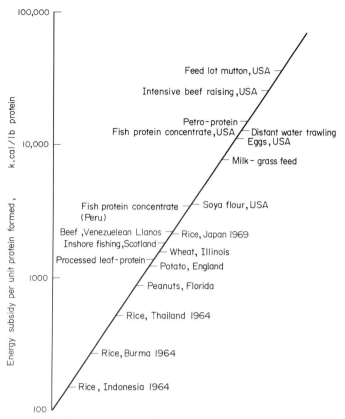

Fig. 9. Typical energy subsidies in modern protein production.

the past. No dramatic improvement can be expected in the short term; and again we must stress that it is in those countries, or many of them, that population increase will be greatest. Present world population around 4 billion will have increased to around 6.5 billion by 2000 and will reach 12 billion in 2075 according to UN estimates. By the year 2000, the United States, Canada, Australia and New Zealand are likely to be the important net exporters of food, even more than today, and the main importers will be Third World countries.

The IFIAS programme on "Food and Fuel Self-Reliance" aims at examining the technical and socio-cultural conditions for a more self-reliant and decentralized production of food and energy in the developing countries. By self-reliance is meant satisfaction of food and fuel needs to be able to meet basic human requirements at the national level.

3. RESOURCE AVAILABILITY

(1) Land and Vegetation

Extension of agricultural production raises the question of the availability of suitable land. At first sight the prospects seem good, since it appears that only 10% of the total land surface of the earth is used for food production and the UN World Plan of Action projection for 1985 suggests a "relatively modest" gain of 600 million hectares or double the area of available land utilized in 1962. It is estimated that a fourth of the world's available land organized to maximum efficiency of yield would be able to supply food for several times the present population. However, the best land is already in use and as poorer and poorer soils come into agricultural use the costs increase enormously. It is calculated that of the total land economically viable for agriculture, 47% is already in use in North America, 63% in Europe and 74% in Latin America. Some of these figures may be even higher as Table 6 suggests.

of fertilizers, weed killers and other chemicals. This may well be a too pessimistic view, but the situation is serious and warrants urgent review and analysis.

It was clear from the reports by the participants from fifteen countries who attended the IFIAS workshop in Samarkand in June 1976 that the rate of degradation of agriculturally productive soils in most parts of the world is very alarming. Besides partial degradation of soils and decrease of their productivity, much more threatening are the grow-

TABLE 6
Arable and Cultivated Land and Population, Worldwide

| Region | Population in 1975 (millions) | Land area (million km²) | | | Cultivated area per person (hectares) | Cultivated land as % of potentially arable land |
		Total	Potentially arable	Cultivated		
Africa	401	30.2	7.33	1.58	0.39	22
Asia	2255	27.3	6.28	5.18	0.23	82
Australia and New Zealand	17	8.2	1.54	0.16	0.94	10
Europe	473	4.8	1.74	1.54	0.33	89
North and Central America	316	21.1	4.66	2.39	0.76	51
South America	245	17.5	6.80	0.77	0.31	11
USSR	255	22.3	3.56	2.27	0.89	64
Total	3967	131.5	31.9	13.89	0.35	43

Note: Cultivated area is called by FAO "arable land and land under permanent crops". It includes land under crops, land temporarily fallow, temporary meadows for mowing or pasture, market and kitchen gardens, fruit trees, vines, shrubs, and rubber plantations. Within this definition there are said to be wide variations among reporting countries. The land actually harvested during any particular year is about one-half to two-thirds of the total cultivated land. Populations of some islands omitted.
Source: For population: *1975 Population Data Sheet,* Population Reference Bureau, Inc., Washington, DC. For land: President's Science Advisory Committee, *The world food problem,* Economic Research Service, United States Department of Agriculture, Foreign agricultural economic report 298, Government Printing Office, Washington, DC, 1974.

At present, moreover, much good land is going out of cultivation to provide for urban expansion, roads, runways, etc., while there is already considerable alarm about the loss of soil quantity and quality through over-grazing, erosion, salinization, etc. It is even said that we have already lost an estimated 60% of the world's top soil once available to man and that the rest is deteriorating because of the over-use

ing areas of fully destroyed and alienated soils which were productive earlier. The extent of salinization, alkalinization, erosion, acidization, pulverization, compaction, and petrification of soils can be so great in places that their fertility will be fully lost. Examples of such destruction are plentiful in Asia, Africa, Australia, Europe, North and South America and the Near East.

According to the Soviet soil expert, Professor Victor Kovda of Moscow University, the total area of destroyed and degraded soil which was biologically productive at one time is estimated at two billion hectares, which is 33% higher than the entire arable area cultivated for agricultural purposes at present, estimated to 1.5 billion hectares. But the real net loss and its dynamics at the global level has not yet been carefully determined and weighed against the potentiality of increased productivity. This must thus be an urgent task as a basis for preventive measures and rational practices of land utilization and is also the main purpose of the IFIAS project "Save our Soils"—SOS.

The land situation suggests intensification of agriculture in the existing good lands. According to the authorities this will necessitate an increase in the intensity of use of agricultural land from 0.4 hectares *per capita,* as at present, to 0.2 hectares *per capita* in the year 2000. Energy analysis suggests that the limit here is around 0.1 hectares *per capita,* beyond which the artificial energy substitution becomes prohibitive. There is also much need for reform of the land tenure systems of many countries, consolidation of scattered holdings and the need to organize smallholders as a necessary instrument to achieve larger output. An interesting comparison between high- and low-intensive agriculture for the world's food production has recently been made by P. Buringh and H. D. J. van Heemst at the University of Wageningen in the Netherlands.* The study suggests that the only viable possibility, without disastrous ecological effects, to feed a world population of 6 billion people is high-intensive agriculture on the soils which are most productive today. (See Tables 7 and 8.)

*P. Buringh and H. D. J. van Heemst, *An Estimation of World Food Production Based on Labour-Oriented Agriculture,* 1977.

(2) Forests and Ground Vegetation

The values to human society of healthy forest ecosystems extend far beyond the obvious ones of timber, wood products and recreational resources. In a recent World Bank policy paper, *Forestry,* Sector Policy Paper, World Bank, February 1978, it is stated:

> The consequences of continued uncontrolled forest exploitation are of critical concern to mankind, for they could lead to serious environmental disruption and increased rural poverty. Over 90% of wood consumption in the developing countries is accounted for by fuel wood. Over-exploitation of existing fuel wood resources, exacerbated by the recent energy crisis, is leading, in many areas, to diversion of agricultural residues and dried livestock dung to use for heating and cooking instead of improving soil fertility.

> Although the forest area in developing countries exceeds 1,000 million hectares, it is being consumed at such a rate for agricultural settlement that it could disappear within 60 years—unless some fundamental changes occur to alter the current trend, or unless extensive reforestation programmes are undertaken to offset the losses.

> Forests cover one-third of the land area of the world and over half the land of developing countries. Annual world production of forest products exceeds $115,000 million; global trade amounts to more than $30,000 million. Forests play a significant role in economic development; they provide subsistence, shelter, and employment, as well as resources for development of other sectors.

But removal of temperate-zone forests also results in heavy losses of nutrients from the

TABLE 7
Data of Various Systems of Agriculture

Agricultural system	Cultivated land	Harvested cereal crop land	Average yield	Total cons. food	Available food	Population	Agr. population
	Mha	Mha	kg-ha^{-1}	Mt	b)	M	M
Present	1406	928	1,358	1260[a)	300	4200	2000
Modern (on present agr. land)	1406	928	7,287	5338	800	6673	160
Labour-oriented (66)	2462	1625	1,978	1606	300	5353	2000
Labour-oriented (44)	2462	1083	1,978	1071	300	3570	1350
Labour-oriented (33)	2462	812	1,978	803	300	2677	1000

a) without post harvest losses
b) kg *per caput* per year

TABLE 8
Estimates of Sustainable Population for Different Agricultural Systems
(in millions of persons)

	South Am.	Australia	Africa	Asia	North Am.	Europe	World
Present population 1977[a)	230	20	410	2400	390	750	4200
Modern agr. on present agr. land	474	235	795	3661	890	728	6673
Labour-oriented agr. (66) on maximum agr. land	803	190	787	1420	1303	853	5356
Labour-oriented agr. (44) on maximum agr. land	535	127	525	947	870	570	3574
Labour-oriented agr. (33) on maximum agr. land	401	95	383	710	651	427	2677

a) Based on World Bank population data (1968) and growth rates.

soil. Forest ecosystems exercise considerable control over patterns of climate, hydrology, circulation of nutrients, erosion, the cleansing functions of air and water, as well as over the status of streams, lakes and underground water supplies. Human activities have already substantially reduced the world's forests and produced a great increase in the amount of desert and wasteland. Such destructive activities have accelerated as the human population has increased, and in many cases complex interactions between human beings and the environment have led to ecocatastrophes.

IFIAS is launching a project which will take all these factors into account and aim at devising new patterns of management of the world's forests. The project will be based on case studies in different parts of the world so as to give the widest possible spread in the factors affecting forests and ground vegetation.

(3) Fertilizers

Continuing our consideration of the food situation it would be well to look into the position of fertilizers which constitute yet another critical element. At present, annual world production is about 80 million tons, of which 36 million are nitrogenous fertilizers, 23 million are phosphates and 19 million are potash. There appears to be sufficient phosphate, which is only slowly assimilated, to last for several centuries at present rates of use and potash is probably still more plentiful. The supply of nitrogenous fertilizers may pose great problems owing to the uncertainty of the hydrocarbon base, the cost of the energy involved in manufacturing and the high capital cost of plants, but in the end, as we shall see later, the main constraint in their use may be the threat to the environment. FAO and other sources estimate that today's real needs are about 150 million tons of fertilizer per annum, i.e. about twice the present world production

and if the average European use of 200 kg. per hectare, per year, were generally applied, this would demand about twice this quantity, which is not too unrealistic considering the need to intensify agriculture in the Third World. High capital requirement could be a limiting factor—a 1,500 ton per day plant represents an investment of about two hundred million dollars. Even at a price of $200 per ton, which the poor countries can ill afford, such plants offer little incentive for investment. A minimum of 100 such plants are needed in the next few years, but there are no signs that this is likely to happen. Lester Brown* has estimated that the total capital investment needed to face the world food shortage between now and the end of the century would be four times all investments in fertilizer production in this century. We may well ask also what would be the effect on soil quality, if this enormous amount of chemicals was in fact to be used. In any case, we have to remember that the efficiency of plant growth for each increment increase of fertilization obeys the law of diminishing returns.

(4) Water

Water is one of the essential elements of human life and civilization. We are dependent for our existence on the gigantic solar-driven hydrological distillation system, within which water from the oceans is evaporated, circulated through the planetary wind system, distributed to the continents, over which it is precipitated in the form of rain or snow which interact with the soil, rocks and vegetation. Some of it remains in underground basins, but most of it is drained off and finds itself in the rivers from which it returns to the oceans, thus closing the cycle.

While water availability has always been the critical factor in desert and arid lands, in the

*L. Brown, *By Bread Alone,* Northon 1974.

temperate regions where it has hitherto been plentiful, it is regarded as a "free good", not necessarily to be taken into account in the economic balance sheets, and used freely to supply the needs of men and animals, agriculture and industry, for power production, fisheries, and for recreation. With the enormous increase in human activity, which we have noted, the indefinite availability of cheap water supplies can no longer be taken for granted and shortfalls are beginning to appear, while in many parts of the less developed world, population increase will inevitably make increasing demands on what has been regarded as a scarce resource from the beginning of human history. Particular problems are likely to arise from the increasing extent of urbanization and it will be difficult and expensive to fill the needs of the considerable numbers of huge cities which are likely to mushroom during the next few decades.

Man has already begun to modify water circulation and quality in many ways—quantitatively by the withdrawal of large quantities of water for irrigation and industrial purposes, also by the regulation and diversion of rivers and through the disposal of waste waters from sewage disposal and industrial effluents. It must be realized also that partly through the absence of good practices of hygiene, water in many parts of the world acts as the medium for the transmission of water-borne diseases such as bilharzia, while the danger of harm to health and life in other areas comes from the toxic chemicals carried.

Furthermore, there are many indirect human interventions on the water system, especially through modification of the soil cover and the density and nature of vegetation and generally by changes in the land-use pattern. Deterioration in the quality of water carried effluents can also give rise to ecological disturbances such as eutrophication.

In fact water, as one of the strands of the *problématique* is intimately connected to many social, economic and cultural factors and it is less and less possible to plan for its management on simple demand considerations in isolation from the local and general patterns of culture and social behaviour.

Water is considered by many as the most critical of all the world's resources, more so even than energy, and may well become the limiting factor for development in many parts of the world. Water can be developed and utilized on a sustained basis within the constraints imposed by the natural hydrological cycle, which operates on an enormous scale through evaporation and precipitation. The hydrological cycle, which transfers enormous quantities of mass and some energy in space, exhibits also temporal aspects such as yearly periods and long-term trends and cycles. These two sets of attributes—of space and time—are at the root of the central problem in water resources development and use, i.e. the discrepancy between the demand for and availability of water. The total run-off of water available on a global basis is estimated at 46×10^{12} m^3/year (on the average)* which, assuming an adequate standard of living requiring 5,000 m^3 *per capita* per year would suffice for a population of over 8 billion people. (See Fig. 10.) It must be realised also that a large proportion of the world's water, in the oceans and elsewhere, is salt and that a further enormous quantity lies frozen in the icecaps. Of all water on earth, some 99.3% is contained in the oceans and the ice caps (Table 9).

The uses of water cover a broad range of activities. Foremost is the consumption of water for the maintenance of the delicate thermochemical balances within the human body. This in itself amounts to relatively small quantities of water, for even under extreme conditions of heat, dryness and physical exertion, man

*M. I. Budyko, *Climate and Life,* Academic Press, New York, 1974.

TABLE 9
Average Water Balance of the Continents

	Precipitation (cm/yr)	Evaporation (cm/yr)	Run off	
			(cm/yr)	(km³/yr)
Africa	69	43	26	7,700
Asia	60	31	29	13,000
Australia	47	42	5	380
Europe	64	39	25	2,200
North America	66	32	34	8,100
South America	163	70	93	16,600

Source: P. R. Ehrlich, A. H. Ehrlich, J. P. Holdren, *Ecoscience,* W. H. Freeman, 1977

seldom needs more than about five litres per day.

However, as standards of living rise and societies become more complex, the use of water *per capita* increases. The amount of water used in cities increased by a factor of seven between 1900 and 1960, and by 1980 is expected to reach twelve times the 1960 level.

Large amounts of water are diverted for food production—about half the total usage of water today. Water is conveyed not only to intensively cultivated lands under irrigation, but also to extensive areas where partial (supplementary) irrigation may make the difference between good crop yields and practically no yield at all. About 0.5m³ of water is necessary to produce one kilogram of dry weight of cereals. Table 10 gives the water requirements for some products and processes.

Regarding industry, relatively little water is finally incorporated in the industrial product, with the partial exception of the food industry. Manufacturing industry uses water primarily for the removal of its wastes, either material or in the form of heat. For example, one ton of steel requires about 100 m³ of water for its manufacture and a ton of paper approximately twice this amount. All thermal power stations, whether coal-fired, or nuclear, demand immense quantities of water for cooling.

And yet, water, unlike many other natural resources, is amenable to recycling so that in many industrialized regions water is recycled several times in its course between the source and the sea, flowing through people, animals and plants, irrigating fields, removing waste, being purified through bio-chemical processes, circulating through heat exchangers and taking part in chemical processes. Thus the central problem of water resources development and utilization is—in addition to that of the temporal and areal discrepancy between desirability and availability—almost as important as that of water quality (mineral, biological, thermal, etc.) and of the management of water systems based on an adequate organizational structure. The over-all problem is, therefore, partly of an engineering-technological nature and partly socio-political and managerial.

Although, on a global basis, it seems that fresh water is still in ample supply, the great geographical variability brings it about that certain regions already use their water at a rate in excess of the natural run-off, while in other places there are large amounts of unused water. If in the latter areas one can expect development and growth to utilize gradually more of their resources, in the former regions water has already become a factor constraining growth and development and non-conventional sources of water are sought. Two such sources may be considered: one based on a process emulating the spectacular desalination system of nature itself; the other making use of the fact that a

TABLE 10
Some Water Requirements

Use	Amount of Water Used (m^3)
Drinking water (adult, daily)	0.001
Toilet (1 flush)	0.02
Clothes washer (1 load)	0.17
Refine a ton of petroleum	2-50
Produce a ton of finished steel	6-270
Grow a ton of wheat	300-500
Grow a ton of rice	1500-2000
Produce a ton of milk	10,000
Produce a ton of beef	20,000-50,000

Source: P. R. Ehrlich, A. H. Ehrlich, J. P. Holdren,
Ecoscience, W. H. Freeman, 1977

very large portion of the world's available fresh water resides as ice in the Antarctic and Greenland. The development of either source—desalination or towing icebergs to irrigate arid lands—requires considerable capital outlays and large amounts of energy. Both sources can be developed only at sea level, so that additional capital and energy is required for the conveyance of water to points of demand, usually situated at higher elevations. Thus water which was formerly regarded as a "free good" becomes an important economic factor in many regions.

The temporal mismatching between supply and demand for water can often be alleviated by storage. Storage of water on the land surface (in reservoirs, behind dams) is becoming more costly. The best available dam sites are already in use and the remaining locations require heavier investments. However, the use of ground water aquifers as storage elements in regional water resources systems may help to solve the problem. The aggregate pore space of aquifers in a region may be several times larger than the available total storage volume on the surface. Aquifers have the additional advantage of not losing water through evaporation, but demand skilled management and input of energy for pumpage.

The connection between water and energy has many aspects. Water is necessary for oil refining and coal mining, and for cooling thermal power plants. Flowing water may have positive energetic aspects (hydropower generation), or negative (soil erosion and sedimentation). And from here, the link to agriculture and food production is quite clear.

The problem of water quality assumes considerable proportions in industrialized regions. The discharge of urban and industrial wastes into water-courses prejudices the water supply of downstream communities and may present a health hazard to them. Technologies, economic incentives and (dis-incentives) and institutional structures were devised to deal with this problem; they met with only partial success. The concept emerging from the impairment of water quality through its use, is that a user of water should be responsible for all outcomes—direct or indirect—brought about by his activities.

All water resources systems, particularly those on a regional scale, have an influence on the environment. An outstanding example in this respect is the Aswan dam which caused considerable ecological dislocation in the Nile river valley and generated drainage, pest control, and fertilizer application problems. As a

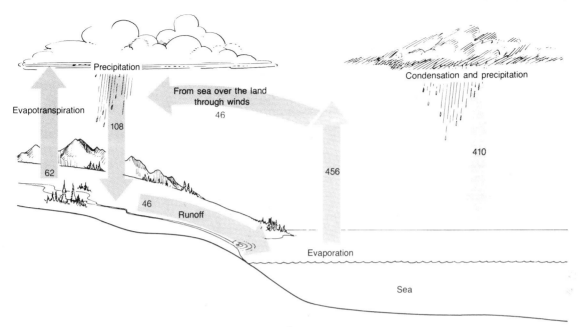

Fig. 10 The hydrologic cycle (1000 km³/yr). (Data from M. I. Budyko, 1974.)

result, the farm production of Egypt actually decreased by 3% since completion of the dam.

The development of water resources for various uses—domestic, agricultural, industrial —followed a pattern similar to Ricardo's law in economics: the sources requiring smaller investments and less effort were developed before the others. As the demand for water increased, costlier sources were brought into use as a response to the supply-demand stress. This stress—or shortage—has two major aspects: quantities of water insufficient for the satisfaction of demands, and the degradation of water quality. On a local or regional basis, water shortage may be caused by inefficiencies of use, where considerable quantities may be lost through seepage and evaporation *en route* from sources to areas of demand. As a result, regional irrigation projects may attain extremely low over-all efficiencies of water use of not more than 25-30%, accompanied by salinization of lands and of groundwater.

A partial solution to the water shortage in agriculture is the improvement of irrigation methods. One such method recently developed effectively in Israel, is drip irrigation, which appears to be biologically highly efficient. An additional solution might be the improvement of the plant genetic material along lines similar to those of the cereal species of the "green revolution": varieties generating more dry matter per unit of irrigation water should be isolated and improved.

As a result of increasing economic activity, standards of living and population increase, acute shortage of water will probably have a significant influence on our life style. Water rationing and complete prohibition of washing of cars have been enforced in various parts of the world for given periods of time. Other prohibitions of use cannot be ruled out. The point is that under conditions of shortage, water use patterns will have to change. Such changes are difficult to bring about because of the resistance to change inherent in most of us.

This is reflected by the fact that the domestic demand for water is inelastic to price or to income, until the water bill amounts to about 3% of the income.

Alleviation of water shortages is attained either through the development of additional water supplies, or through the manipulation of the demand, or by a mix of the two. Either alternative requires considerable capital outlays, which may compete with other development activities.

Summary of World Food Situation

The combination of the factors described above leads to the conclusion that the prospects for world food provision for the next 30-40 years are grim, especially when one considers that hundreds of millions are already starving. Only the maximum possible use of all the various means can free the world from this nightmare of impending famines, and preparations must be made now. Large efforts are, however, made, especially in the developing countries, to raise crop yields, reduce waste and post-harvest losses by improved storage and transportation technology, improve disease and salinity resistance of plants by genetic manipulation, improve biological nitrogen fixation, introduce water-saving irrigation methods, prevent further degradation of productive soils and maybe develop a new type of agricultural science and technology specially adapted to tropical regions for a more self-reliant food production. It is far from certain that the energy and capital intensive agricultural methods being applied in the industrialized countries are appropriate for the LDCs.

(5) Energy

Energy is a fundamental input of life and hence its availability is the key to development. All materials can be regarded as energy in tem-

porarily stable forms and, given sufficient cheap energy, the transformation of materials into others should be possible. Hence, in theory at least, plentiful and cheap energy should obviate material limitations by making substitution possible and should also enable food production to expand almost indefinitely. As long as the sun shines and man is capable of trapping it, radiation energy will be available. In Fig. 11 is presented the qualitative relations between energy and well-being.

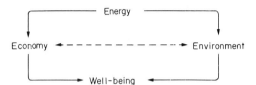

Fig. 11. From P. R. Ehrlich, A. H. Ahrlich and J. P. Holdren, *Ecoscience,* W. H. Freeman, 1977.

The energy resources are practically infinite for all human purposes but tend to become less and less accessible for the different uses in society. The European Community now estimates that for each unit of *useful* energy output 1.35 units of energy input is needed. Some years ago this figure was much lower. So, we might say that the energy for socio-economic purposes is getting increasingly expensive in energy terms and certainly also in monetary terms.

An interesting model of the global energy balance in terms of output of useful energy in relation to energy inputs, has recently been made by Hounam and Slesser.* The very first runs of the model indicate that both industry production *per capita* and energy demands *per capita,* go through a maximum around the years 1990-2000, after which it will be falling.

---

*M. Slesser and I. Hounam, A Global Energy Model (Private communication at IFIAS seminar in Poona on Self-reliance, Oct. 1978).

We have become accustomed to consume the energy of past aeons of solar radiation in the form of fossil fuels, stored in the earth in great, but irrevocably limited, quantities. Furthermore, until recently, these have been available freely and at very low prices. The recent crisis was not really an energy crisis, but essentially a petroleum crisis. It did, however, make evident the need to develop long- term strategies for world energy use and provision. We have indeed been using the cheap and convenient oil and gas for many purposes for which it is by no means essential, for example in the production of low grade heat for space and water heating, chemical processing and the generation of electricity for which many other alternatives are more appropriate and less wasteful. As a consequence much of our apparatus of manufacture is at present geared to the use of petroleum hydrocarbons which are now no longer cheap and, for those industrialized countries which are heavy importers of oil, with considerable uncertainties of continuity of supply.

The estimated life of fossil fuel reserves is not known precisely, owing to uncertainties of future rise in demand and also the unknown extent of new deposits which might be discovered as well as the economies of secondary and tertiary recovery at some later date.

A recent survey* made by Exxon Corporation, shows that during the decade 1967-76, nearly 13,000 exploratory wells were drilled throughout the non-Communist world.

Of 71 countries, where exploratory wells were drilled, 41 showed encouraging results. Of the most recent "super giant" discoveries that have been made during the last decade, that of Mexico is the most significant. It has been estimated to be twice as big as that of Saudi Arabia. On the whole, however, explorations are forced into harsher environments, both politically and geographically, which may slow down and make the process more expensive.

*Exxon Corp. June, 1978 (Private communication).

The price factor is important and will, if we continue to rely essentially on the market forces, have a considerable influence on the intensity of exploration for new deposits of fossil fuels as well as on the tempo of research and development on non-traditional possibilities. For example, it is already clear that the recovery costs to the British of North Sea oil will make that product even more expensive than the present OPEC prices. Meanwhile, industrial development may be stimulated by the accessibility of North Sea oil and the lowering of the pressure on the balance of payments, which the new discoveries should provide, and this could lead to even greater economic difficulties some 25-30 years hence.

In the meantime the high *sales* price of oil could lead to considerable politico-economic disparities. The two super powers are both major producers of oil which, like that of the Middle East countries, has a recovery cost much lower than the sales cost. They will, therefore, have available large quantities of petroleum at real costs which are very much lower than that available to the oil-importing countries such as those of Europe, Japan and the Third World, with consequent influence on relative competitive positions.

With regards to coal, it may be assumed that world reserves are sufficient for several hundred years and, if extended by the use of heavy oils, oil shales and tar sands as cost increase makes the exploitation of such fuels economic, perhaps for five hundred years or more. It must be realized, however, that many of the industrialized nations, where prosperity was initially built on supplies of domestic coal, will run into serious scarcity problems in the next half century. Petroleum, on the other hand, may become scarce in an absolute and not merely political sense in 30-50 years. This figure indicates how salutary the oil crisis has been, when one realises that the lead time for research and development of non-traditional energy sources is very long so that programmes in this direction should be encountered now on a sufficient scale to enable sizable production to begin by the end of the century.

A number of comprehensive surveys on future supply and demand of energy, especially petroleum, have recently been published. It is interesting to note that these studies now all seem to converge on the quantitative estimates of supply/demand ratios.

The most impressive of these studies, the WAES Report,* was the work of an international group of scientists and economists from a large number of countries, including people from the energy industry and governments, led by Professor Carroll L. Wilson of MIT. This study attempts to assess the global prospects for energy up to the year 2000 and, on the basis of statistical data on the many factors involved, to work out a series of alternative scenarios involving different oil price assumptions, economic growth rates, oil production levels and policy responses. The most probable of these indicates a shortfall in energy supply by the 1990s, even on the assumption of a considerable use of fission energy and large energy conservation measures.

Petroleum is at present essential for two quite different purposes, firstly as the basis of the petro-chemical industry for the manufacturing of plastics, synthetic fibres, materials of all sorts, dyestuffs, drugs and the whole range of organic chemicals; secondly to provide the motive force of many means of transportation such as automobiles, aeroplanes and diesel trains. Indeed, we owe it to future generations not to burn up the complex and valuable molecules which nature has constructed and conserved over the ages in the space of barely a century. Yet, of the petroleum products consumed today, some 70% goes to manufacturing industry, only 10% is used in transportation

*Energy: Global Prospects 1985-2000—Report of the Workshop on Alternative Energy Strategies (WAES), MIT Press, Cambridge, Mass., 1977.

and 10% for space heating; the petrochemical industry, as yet consumes a very small fraction. Thus the proportion of the very limited supply of this non-renewable resource used for purposes for which it is uniquely necessary is rather small.

The above figures are valid, of course, mainly for the industrialized countries. Recent comparisons show that the fraction of the total energy consumption required for one unit of GNP-growth is very similar for the industrial sector of most industrialized countries, while the corresponding ratio for the transportation sector varies considerably between these countries. For instance, to produce one unit of GNP-growth twice as much energy is required in the transportation sector in the USA than in the UK.

As far as transport is concerned we can, of course, push railway electrification and return to coal-driven vehicles—although the argument of the need to preserve a basis for organic chemical synthesis applies, though with lesser force, to coal—but the mobility advantages of the internal combustion and jet engines will not be easy to renounce, and will certainly continue for the rest of the century—but not to the polluting and road-cluttering extent of today. Later, if a hydrogen economy is developed or possibly one based on methanol, alternative propellants for the automobile could be made generally available and be less pollutive. Many firms already have quite advanced programmes for methanol or ethanol automobile engines.

The demand pattern for energy for the rest of the century is difficult to foresee. It will depend so much on the extent to which the industrialized countries are desirous or able to maintain their high rates of economic growth and the ability of the Third World to develop and pay for the energy which their food and other needs will demand. Amongst the various scenarios, that of John P. Holdren, which is one of intermediate demand, would foresee a total energy use for a world of 6.7 billion people in

2020, of about four times the 1972 consumption, while other calculations would indicate as much as ten times that of the same base year. The Holdren scenario would bring the energy consumption of the poor nations by 2020 up to about that of Japan or Austria today and of the rich to that of the United States in the early 1960s. It is uncertain whether even his intermediate level would be possible without serious environmental and climatic impact, and indeed recent work on the effects of local concentrations of thermal pollution tend to increase these doubts. A recent report by Elbek,* suggests that the total world energy use in the year 2000, will be 2½ times that of 1978.

In Table 11, the quantitative relations between energy and prosperity for different countries are given. Of special interest are the figures of the energy use in relation to the Gross National Product, GNP. Elbek's very recent analysis reports the following figures:

Low-income countries	55 MJ/$
Middle-income countries	66 MJ/$
High-income countries	33 MJ/$

With present energy systems, Elbek concludes that it seems difficult to come below 22 MJ/$

Within the complex of problems and uncertainties relating to near-term and long-term energy provision and use, a series of quite general questions arise:

—How can we maintain energy supplies to meet rising demand and population increase during the next 30-40 years?
—Are we justified, on economic, environmental and moral grounds in attempting to maintain existing use patterns and, in particular, to meet the ever mounting demands of societies of gluttony and overconsumption?

*Bent Elbek, *World Energy Outlook and Options,* Niels Bohr Institute, University of Copenhagen, Denmark. November, 1978.

—How can we achieve a more sensible and equitable distribution of the different forms of energy, particularly between industrialized and developing countries?
—Is much to be gained through energy conservation and increased efficiency of energy use and what are the costs?
—Can we come through the transition without substantial use of nuclear energy?— without fast breeders?
—What are environmental limits to energy use?
—What research, development and planning should be started now with regard to the provision of energy from non-traditional sources in the early decades of the next century, in view of the long lead-time of the chain of research, development and production on a significant scale?

Near-term perspective

Present lead-times introducing new energy technologies and self-imposed constraints make "near-term" predictions easy. It takes little expertise to predict what we are *not* going to have in the next 10 years. The dominant near-term options are:

—Oil and Natural Gas;
—Conservation;
—Coal;
—Nuclear Fission Energy.

Oil and Natural Gas will continue to be burned at an accelerated rate and at rising costs. The fact that we will have a relative glut of petroleum and gas during the next few years makes it very difficult politically to implement any plan for conservation and to introduce alternative energy sources. Recent events in the USA makes this evidently clear. More than 40% of the American people do not even know that the USA is importing petroleum in very large quantities (7 million barrels per day) at present. In all industrialized countries life styles

TABLE 11
Energy Use and GNP in Selected Countries, 1973

Country	Annual energy consumption *per capita* (MJ)	Equivalent GNP *per capita* ($US)	MJ/$	Net imports of energy (% of consumption)*
United States	344,000	6200	55	11
Czechoslovakia	193,000	2870	67	19
East Germany	180,000	3000	60	22
Sweden	176,000	5910	30	90
United Kingdom	166,000	3060	54	47
West Germany	167,000	5320	31	50
Netherlands	175,000	4330	40	37
USSR	142,000	2030	70	NE†
Switzerland	108,000	6100	18	80
Japan	104,000	3630	29	98
New Zealand	92,900	3680	25	58
Argentina	55,000	1640	34	12
Mexico	39,000	890	44	3
China, People's Republic	16,300	270	60	2
Brazil	16,300	760	21	54
Egypt	8,500	250	34	NE
India	5,400	120	45	18
Indonesia	3,800	130	29	NE
Nigeria	1,900	210	9	NE

Note: Excludes wood, dung, agricultural residues, food.
*1971.
†NE = net exporter.
Sources: UN, *Statistical yearbook;* World Bank, *Atlas.*

are conducive to large waste of energy and there is little evidence that the considerable price rise of petroleum since the recent "crisis" has done much to cut, for example, the excessive use and abuse of the automobile.

Conservation measures, including better insulation of buildings and factories, higher energy efficiency of industrial production processes, and slightly lower speeds for automobiles on the highways, are desirable but involve considerable capital investments to society and individuals and it is a rather lengthy process. Higher fuel costs, e.g., by increased taxes, will encourage this but we can probably expect only moderate success.

Considerable savings could be obtained in the transportation sector through the development of more efficient and convenient public transportation systems, for which many in-teresting possibilities exist and by siting future industrial complexes and offices so as to enable the work-force to live within reasonable distance from the places of work. The energy question of this is linked with that of urban development. The so called "new towns" in England represent a promising development. In some of these towns the settlement arrangement is such that only one of ten trips which the inhabitants must make between their living quarters and the job locations or service centres is longer than one and a half kilometres.

The IFIAS pilot study of Denmark* shows that some 30% of all energy used in the Danish economy can be saved by appropriate conservation measures in all sectors of the economy, if a

Energy in Denmark 1990-2005, A Case Study, Summary of Study, Niels Bohr Inst. of Physics, Copenhagen, Denmark, 1976.

sufficiently long time perspective, i.e. 10 years, is used for the necessary capital investments. (See Fig. 12.) Such a policy would have a significant effect on the Danish balance of trade by the reduced oil import. The use of traditional technologies and no changes of life style were assumed for the Danish pilot study.

Over the next 10 years maybe 15-20% of the total energy consumption could be saved by conservation measures in the industrialized countries. However, conservation can be made only once, and it costs energy as well as capital. Energy conservation seems to come slowly because it implies regulation, fiscal control, and bureaucratic interference in the freedom of choice. It is important, however, because it buys time for solving other energy problems, like that of the threats to world peace by proliferation of nuclear technology and that of the development of alternative sources. Energy conservation is necessary and may even have a significant impact on our health.

The range of the viable energy resources is likely to be much greater than in the past but will depend greatly on the cost of petroleum. Certainly a greater effort in the mining and use of *Coal* is required and this will entail considerable social problems, especially of attracting a substantial labour force to the mines in a period of generally high living standards in many countries and of the social need to enhance work satisfaction and good conditions of labour. In the United States extensive mechanization is possible; in Europe this is much more difficult as the coal strata are much thinner. Intensification of development of new methods of mechanization is required as well as new approaches such as underground gasification. It is probable, too, that much advance will be made with regard to the manufacture of high calorific oil and gases from coal, although they have a high capital outlay, if it is to contribute a significant proportion to demand. The use of oil shales, tar sands, etc., is likely to be developed in the later years of the century. As

we shall see later, the environmental dangers in burning much greater quantities of carbon compounds is great although quantitatively uncertain, and, in a future energy strategy, this will have to be considered seriously.

The choice of energy sources appropriate for a given use is an important problem and there may well be a tendency to restrict petroleum to the essential uses we have mentioned and to reconvert much of the manufacturing capacity to use other forms of energy. In particular it will be desirable to make further use of low-grade heat such as that from electricity and nuclear stations for town heating and chemical manufacture and to improve the efficiency of many uses by means of the heat pump.

There seems to be a broad consensus around the world that even if all obstacles to vigorous government energy policies were eliminated to implement conservation on a large scale, to expand oil and gas production, hydropower, and alternative energy sources such as coal, solar and geothermal, *Nuclear Fission Energy* will still be necessary on a large scale if the industrialized world is to make a smooth transition to a sustainable energy future dominated by renewable resources.

Within the nuclear fission option there are many alternatives. The Light Water Reactor System and the Canadian heavy water reactor (CANDU) are already economically competitive and their technologies are well understood. Other practical or potentially practical alternatives are the boiling water reactors, high temperature gas reactors, and the controversial fast breeder reactors which not only generate heat but also by the reaction of fast neutrons, produce more energy than they consume. The traditional light and heavy water reactors are thermal reactors operating with thermal neutron energy. The fast breeder, in converting non-fissionable "natural" uranium by fast neutron bombardment to plutonium which is fissionable, thus permits the use of most of the natural uranium. It is thus capable

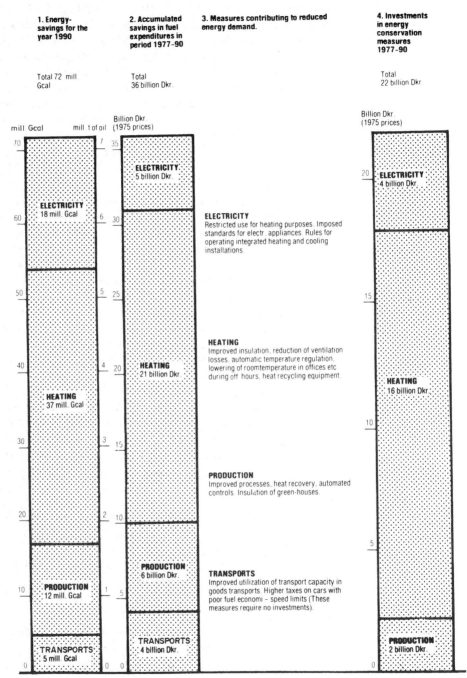

Fig. 12. Survey of energy savings in the period 1977-1990.

of extending uranium supplies about fifty times as compared with the present thermal fission processes. The doubts concerning the use of fast breeders concern the safety of the process itself with its high temperatures and liquid metal coolants and still more important than its product, plutonium is very poisonous and is immediately usable as bomb material.

There are several important questions which seem to be clouding the future of the nuclear energy potential:

> —risks of proliferation of nuclear bomb potential,
> —safety of nuclear reactors,
> —sabotage or terrorism,
> —waste disposal,
> —uncertainty about total uranium resources.

It is not possible in the scope of this short report to discuss each of these in detail in a way they warrant, but it is necessary to make a few comments. Fig 13 shows the nuclear fuel cycle for light-water reactors.

The *proliferation* of nuclear bomb capability is a very complicated issue indeed. There seems to be a fair consensus that the issue is mainly a political-strategic question and not a technical problem of choice of fuel cycles, reprocessing technologies, etc. Any country with a Light Water Reactor can achieve a nuclear bomb potential over a period of one to two years, if it so decides, with a relatively modest investment. India did it with a rather old-fashioned reactor which they had built themselves with only some support from the outside.

Furthermore, new and very efficient isotope separation techniques are developed vigorously in many countries and some of these seem to be easier and cheaper to deploy than a nuclear reactor + reprocessing plant to obtain bomb-grade material.

In the above sense one might say that the proliferation has already reached the point of no return.

What then are the options? What can be done?

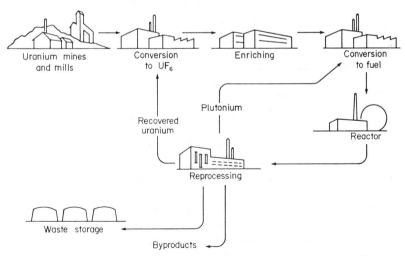

Fig. 13. The nuclear fuel cycle for light-water reactors. Reprocessing, recycle of uranium and plutonium, and final waste-storage steps were not yet in regular operation as of early 1977. (From US Energy Research and Development Administration, 1975.)

There seems to be only one *technical* way out of the proliferation dilemma, and that is to phase out the nuclear alternative completely. But it is politically and economically unrealistic to do this over the next 20 years, which is the minimum time the industrialized countries need for the transition to a sustainable energy mode of operation based on other, and preferable, renewable sources.

Even if the existence of the breeder is not the sole means which permits the proliferation of bomb grade material, the whole issue has become focused on the processing plants for the breeder programme on an international scale.

It is argued that if the world's energy demand continues to grow at the anticipated rate, i.e. approximately 3% for the industrialized countries and 5-6% for the underdeveloped countries, the electricity demand in the year 2000 will be about 8,000 gigawatts, corresponding to 8,000 nuclear power stations of 1,000 MW each. If all these reactors were non-breeders some one thousand million (10^9) tons of uranium ore would have to be mined per year, which seems unacceptable from the environmental point of view. Therefore, it is argued, plutonium is necessary. If the breeders were to take over the whole energy supply, approximately 40 tons of plutonium would have to be processed every day in the year 2000.

The entire question, however, of the need for breeders or not seems to depend on the accessible reserves of uranium and as long as there exists such strongly diverse views on this issue, the breeder question will remain open. Whatever the final stand on the breeder will be, however, the further expansion of nuclear energy technology must try to balance three factors from the political and public opinion point of view, namely Proliferation, Resilience, and Safety.

For all three it is necessary to start moving towards an international institutional system which can handle all factors. But there is no historical evidence of a reasonable longevity of such institutional infrastructures. Furthermore, many argue that the complex and extensive security measures which would be necessary would entail serious curtailment of liberty. Not surprising, therefore, that the energy issue as a whole and the nuclear problem in particular is very confused.

Finally a few words about *safety and waste disposal* problems related to nuclear energy.

The *safety* against burn-outs by sudden loss of coolant for the nuclear fuel assembly, leakage of radioactivity, conventional accidents, or sabotage can be improved by concentrating the reactors in very big technical complexes, so called nuclear parks, instead of spreading the nuclear power stations to many places. In Canada such a park is being created at the Pickering power station which presently contains four 500 MW units, and in the near future there will be an additional four units. The Canadian experience is reported to be good. Such nuclear parks could afford to have sufficient technical and other expertise to handle promptly practically any safety risk or accident.

However, the safety problem is not so much a technical issue as a socio-psychological one. The concept of a 5.10^{-5} "*a priori* probability" for an accident per reactor-year is not understood by the general public. Rather it is the *consequences* of one such accident, *if* it should happen, that frightens people. And the entire question of safety and huge technological units is an important aspect of the resilience of modern society to technical, socio-economic and political changes. Table 12 gives the consequences of the worst-case hypothetical light water reactor (LWR) accident.

The *waste disposal* of increasing quantities of long-lived radioactivity is certainly not yet solved but most likely, satisfactory technical solutions can be found if the development work is continued. But again, this is more a political and public opinion question than a technical question. It is obvious that both the safety and

TABLE 12
Consequences of Worst-case Hypothetical LWR Accident as Estimated by the Rasmussen Report

Effect	Rate or number	Duration	Total number, Rasmussen best estimate	Uncertainty range, multiplicative	Total number, Rasmussen low estimate	Total number, Rasmussen high estimate
Prompt deaths	3,300	—	3,300	$\frac{1}{4}$-4	825	13,200
Cancer deaths	1,500/yr	30-40 yr	45,000- 60,000	$\frac{1}{6}$ -3	7,500	180,000
Prompt illnesses	49,500	—	49,500	$\frac{1}{4}$-4	12,375	198,000
Thyroid illnesses	8,000/yr	30-40 yr	240,000-320,000	$\frac{1}{3}$-3	80,000	960,000
Genetic effects	190/yr	many generations*	28,500	$\frac{1}{6}$ -6	4,750	171,000
Property damage	$14 billion	—	$14 billion	$\frac{1}{5}$ -2	$2.8 billion	$28 billion

*Equivalent to 150 years at constant rate
Source: US Nuclear Regulatory Commission, *Reactor safety study.*

waste disposal issues make the nuclear energy proponents nervous, because the public opinion pressures have disclosed how many of the problems are still unsolved as major national programmes for nuclear power generation go ahead.

For the near- and medium-term perspective at least two things must be implemented as soon as possible:

(1) Devise an international framework which will enable all non-nuclear weapons states which want to (must?) satisfy their energy needs with nuclear power to do so, while minimizing the risks of nuclear weapons proliferation and interfering to the minimum possible extent in favour of the individual.

(2) Help those developing countries which cannot—or will not—embark on a nuclear energy programme to satisfy their energy needs by other alternatives, such as solar, bioconversion, hydropower, geothermal, and coal.

The dilemma behind the nuclear question is that the threats to world peace may be much greater by *not* providing adequate energy for development to all in time than by uncontrolled proliferation of nuclear energy where it is wanted.

For the Third World countries the energy problem is grave. Much of the natural generating capacity will have to be reserved for the life and death attack on agricultural intensification through the manufacture of fertilizers, etc., and restriction of oil consumption to essential uses, such as transportation and the operation of farm machinery. A major effort must be made to provide local and individual systems of electricity generation for lighting, cooking, refrigeration and airconditioning. Wind power may prove useful and economic in some regions, while by the end of the period considerable use will probably be made of the simpler forms of solar energy conversion such as the use of solar stoves, stills, furnaces and refrigeration. There is also scope for efficient conversion of human, animal and agricultural wastes to methane or other fuels.

IFIAS is presently carrying out a project on Food and Fuel Self-reliance which, by pilot studies in developing countries, will test the extent to which modern biological science and technology can help them to become more self-reliant.

Threats of limitation of petroleum supplies have shocked some of the industrialized countries as a lapse from international solidarity. There are, however, many undertones to this which merit sympathetic understanding. Norway, for example, is unwilling to exploit its North Sea oil much more quickly than its domestic and external economic demands would suggest. To increase production would certainly raise prosperity levels, but at considerable social cost, the import of foreign workers and considerable changes in the quality of life, not to be desired. Furthermore the oil reserves being finite, the post-oil period might prove to be exceedingly difficult. For many of the Middle East oil producers the post-oil period will be still more difficult in that they possess very few alternative resources for continuing prosperity other than solar energy. It is not surprising that some of these countries are already beginning to question whether they are right in providing the basis for the wasteful consumption of the industrialized world despite the very large resources this provides at present for national development or foreign investment. Would it not be better for them to prolong life of their oil reserves, especially as its price may well be very high in later years and in view of present levels of inflation? This is not just a long-term or theoretical question. Iran, for example, is assuming in its long-term developing plans, that its export of petroleum twenty years hence is likely to be zero and was planning to introduce nuclear power as the take-over after the year 2000.

Long-term perspective

Many possibilities and options exist for the long-term perspective. For of all, petroleum and natural gas will continue to play a significant role in 15 to 30 years from now. Synthetic gas and crude from coal can also be expected to contribute on a large scale. Other alternatives, such as fast breeders and/or converters, solar, fusion, geothermal, and wave energy of oceans, necessitate massive efforts of research and development, the scale of which will determine their degree of contribution to the total energy supply. For a time perspective of 25-50 years it is of course much more uncertain to predict the contributions from different sources. The most likely candidates, however, are solar and geothermal energy in different forms, breeders, converters, and fusion.

Solar energy has some very striking advantages at a first look. It is infinitely abundant, clean and rather uniformly distributed over the earth's surface. (See Fig. 14.) But it comes down to scale when its dilute nature, coupled with its intermittency, undermines the simplistic view that it is an ideal energy source "since it is delivered at no cost to where the user is". This is not to say that solar energy will not be important but it may take many years before it is economically competitive with synthetic gas and crude and with nuclear power.

The great challenge of solar energy is the many modes by which it can potentially be used, i.e. thermal conversion, direct conversion for electricity production, bioconversion, thermal gradients in the sea, wind, etc. (See Fig. 15 and Table 13.) The role of solar energy is certainly both cost sensitive and dependent on the research devoted to it. But economic criteria are not absolute. Some people will choose—and do already—solar heating and power for other than economic reasons.

Bioconversion will probably play a significant role, especially for the developing countries. Once again the possibilities are great. After all, through the processes of photosynthesis, in which the sun's energy is able to combine through the chlorophyl of the green plant, carbon dioxide from the air and water, carbohydrates are produced corresponding to some 17 times the total world demand for energy. Thus the use of forest and agricultural wastes, and the cultivation of new quick growing species of trees, hold out possibilities of substantial contribution to the world's energy needs. The IFIAS programme on "Self-reliance", mentioned above, is aiming at an in-

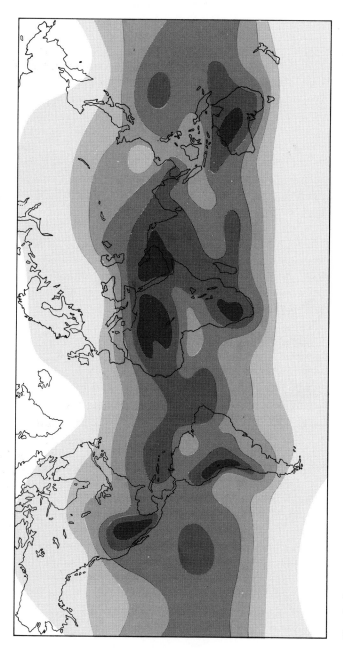

Megajoules per square metre per year

| 2-3000 | 3-4000 | 4-5000 | 5-6000 | 6-7000 | 7-8000 | over 8000 |

Fig. 14. Annual average solar radiation.

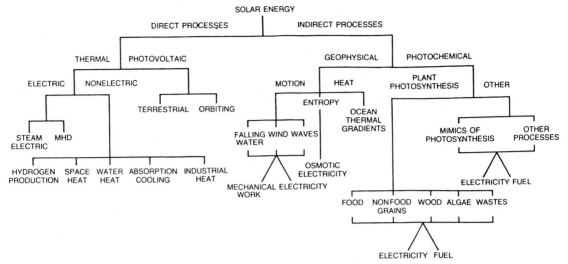

Fig. 15. Options for harnessing solar energy. There are many possibilities. Excluded here are fossil fuels, which
are solar energy stored in chemical form over millions of years.
MHD = magnetohydrodynamics.

TABLE 13
Potential Uses of Sunlight

Low temperature heat (below 150°C)
Crop drying; greenhouses; space heating and cooling; water
distillation, salt production

High temperature heat (up to 600°C)
Water pumps for irrigation; small engines, solar cookers;
process heat (dry or wet); electricity generation by steam
generator

Very high temperatures (above 600°C—experimental at this
stage)
Solar furnaces; manufacture of exotic materials, ceramics;
materials research

Photovoltaic conversion
Water pumps for irrigation; small power supplies (for
example buoys); low-power domestic needs (lighting);
isolated power stations; power sources for space craft

Photosynthetic conversion
Solid fuels (wood); liquid fuel (pyrolysis or hydrogenation
of organic matter); gaseous fuel (anaerobic digestion of
vegetation); chemical feedstocks

tegrated approach to optimal solar energy
utilization for food and energy production in
developing countries for which this is probably
the only way to reduce their strong energy
dependence on other countries.

Nuclear Breeders and Converter reactors
lend themselves to base load supply which solar
energy does not. The need for breeders and/or
converters is dependent on the magnitude of
uranium resources, as was mentioned above,

but also on the total amount of energy needed to carry the whole world over to a state of sustainable energy equilibrium based on renewable resources and fusion. The truth is, however, that no realistic quantitative estimate has yet been made of the global energy need taking into account the deployment of solar energy, conservation, increasing self-reliance of developing countries, and changes of life-styles in industrialized countries. Breeders and/or converters should therefore be seen as an insurance policy for the base load supply. And they are already technically feasible and economically competitive, but the social acceptance is doubtful.

Nuclear Fusion has been regarded as the great hope of the twenty-first century and has been considered as the ultimate resource created by man since the sources of tritium and deuterium in the oceans are practically infinite. Fusion research both through magnetic containment of plasma and by laser induction has made significant progress during the last few years. The scientific problems are now understood and pilot units with net energy gain can be built within the next 5 to 10 years both in the USA, the USSR and Europe, provided the necessary research effort is devoted to it.

It must be noted, however, that the research and development costs are estimated to be as high as $50 billion over the next 15-20 years and with the long lead times involved it is unlikely that fusion will make a significant contribution to electricity supply before about 50 years. Capital costs of constructing reactors are also expected to be high.

Fusion energy is produced by a number of mechanisms similar to that which continually generate the sun's radiation. It takes place at the enormously high temperature of about $1.5 \times 10^{8}°C$ and the engineering problem of utilizing this for electricity generation through steam turbines is at a very early stage. Both magnetically contained plasma and laser-induced fusion seem to be amenable to a hybrid principle in which its high energy neutrons are captured in a blanket of fertile material such as natural uranium which is thus converted to fissile material for use in normal fission reactors. This fusion generation of energy, long thought of as a "clean" process, may still involve the radioactive hazards of conventional nuclear energy which society is not fully willing to accept. In addition , tritium radioactivity still presents problems. If new engineering methods could be developed for the conversion of heat at the very high temperatures of the fusion reactors to a manageable level, the prospects would be much more attractive, but the engineering problems are formidable.

Other energy alternatives

When discussing alternatives other than those presented above it is worth emphasizing that the supply/demand "gap" according to all studies made will correspond to one North Sea or one Alaska per year in the year 2000.

An interesting possibility is offered by *geothermal energy* in different forms. There are six types of geothermal energy which have any significance, i.e. dry steam; hot water; low enthalpy water (exploited mainly in Iceland and Hungary); geopressure zones (45 countries); hot drival areas; and magma energy. Experts on geothermal energy claim that this energy alternative is highly underestimated. The most serious obstacles to wide exploitation of geothermal energy seem to be:
- —lack of knowledge;
- —lack of experts;
- —low research funding;
- —lack of legislation for its use on a large scale.

Dry steam and *hot water* are already economically feasible. The most recent and spectacular finding seems to be *geopressure zones*. In April 1977 an enormous source of mixed methane and water was found in Louisiana, USA. The temperature of the mixture was 420°F and this source alone has been reported to correspond to 2×10^{12} tons of coal. The global potential of energy from geopressure zones seems enormous but we still know much too little about its technical characteristics.

Hot drival area means that two very deep (3,000 metres or more) holes are drilled, each to somewhat different depths. Water which is pumped down into one of the holes is taken out from the other hole at a higher temperature. Promising experiments are being carried out at Los Alamos in New Mexico, USA, with as high as 85% recovery of the injected water as steam. Presently 20,000 KW is produced at *one* such site.

Magma energy alone could, according to the experts, produce one thousand times (1000^x) more electricity than the USA is using at present. But for the time being only one country —Iceland—is carrying out serious research on Magma energy.

Wind energy is one form of solar energy that in some parts of the world may play an important role. However, it is strongly localized and the environmental impacts of thousands of big rotor units are not yet well understood.

Finally, a *tidal wave* power station has existed for many years in France and the dynamic wave energy of oceans is extracted with moderate success in a number of pilot projects in the world. In both cases, capital costs are high and technical problems considerable.

In *summary* the following energy issues stand out as the most important for international policy making:
—The world energy demand will increase strongly as the standard of living and the size of presently disadvantaged populations increase over the next several decades.
—Failure to meet this demand may result in extensive social evils such as poverty, starvation, unrest, epidemics, riots, and maybe even wars.

—No single energy technology can meet the world's future demand. It is likely that all technologies, such as conventional fossil, nuclear fission, nuclear fusion, solar, and geothermal technologies, will be required to meet the qualitative and quantitative needs.
—Each country or region will have to make its own optimal blend of energy technologies, but most of the solutions to the technical as well as political problems of energy must be found within a global framework and by international cooperation.
—An international system must be created which can help all countries to develop their energy sources needed for continued economic growth while minimizing the risks for proliferation of nuclear bomb material.
—The long-term climatic effects of increased energy production should be studied by international programmes.
—Human settlements and transportation systems must be designed to maximize contacts and comfort while minimizing energy usage.
—The industrialized countries must help the less developed countries to develop alternative energy sources with the least negative impacts on culture and ecosystems.

(6) Materials

Mineral ores still exist in the earth in great quantities and although certain chemical elements may well become scarce in the next decades, substitution and recycling possibilities exist to such an extent that they should not, at least in technical terms, represent a real barrier to development.

It is necessary at the outset to destroy the myth that such raw materials exist mainly in the less developed countries and that they are exploited by the industrialized nations. Countries such as Australia, Canada, the Soviet Union and the United States are amongst the greatest producers of minerals while, at the other extreme, the poorest of the poor amongst nations possess practically no mineral resources. Of course no country is completely self-sufficient over the whole range of useful minerals and international trade in these will inevitably continue. Many of the European countries, and—to a spectacular extent—Japan, are very poor in such resources and must rely heavily on imports from other developed nations, as well as from the Third World. Several important minerals, however, lie mainly outside the industrialized countries, particularly copper ores, tin and phosphates.

Some chemical elements are indeed in short supply and may be nearing exhaustion, such as mercury, helium, silver, to some extent tin, while uranium could become difficult in a nuclear, non-breeder economy. However, the substitution of most of these should give rise to no insuperable problems. Helium and silver are perhaps exceptions; the former, because no other inert gases are likely to be available to replace it, and the latter, because silver-salts are still the only generally satisfactory photosensitive materials. For the other metals, substitutions should be easy. In general, as a particular ore becomes scarce, price rises coupled with technological developments bring alternatives into the economic range. Thus not too considerable increases in the price of bauxite may well force the use, by different processes, of clays which are in indefinite supply. We should not, however, be too complacent. As currently used world deposits become exhausted, it will be necessary to move to reserves at higher cost either as a consequence of being of lower grade or because of the need for more complicated extraction processes. Thus there will be technical as well as economic reasons for constantly upward trend in prices. An example is the increasing cost of mining and extraction of gold in South Africa, a technical factor with

economic impact, because of the continuing function of gold as a monetary standard. Fig. 16 shows the global supplies and demands for some selected minerals.

Such trends also involve, as a rule, greater expenditure of energy. It is expected, for instance, that the copper ores generally exploited a decade hence will cost about double in energy per unit of copper recovered, as compared with those in use today. At the same time, environmental costs mount. Already in the beneficiation of copper ores, there are about 400 tons of waste rock to be removed for each ton of copper extracted. With still lower grade ores, material handling and beneficiation costs and the vast amount of rock to be disposed of represent future energy and environmental costs.

The prolongation of metal supplies can of course be assured by recycling of scrap and by the design, manufacture and sale of products with a much longer life. It is estimated that even today some 55% of the copper put into use is recycled. Increasing prices of the virgin material will certainly encourage a much greater extent of recycling than is the case today.

The IFIAS project on Energy Analysis is relevant to many of these considerations. It is extremely important for manufacturers, economists and the public to be aware of the energy contained in a whole variety of materials and products, with rising costs. This may well encourage a change in the pattern of industry towards the use of lower energy-hungry materials and also have an influence on the orientation of research and development. For example, aluminium is a highly energy-intensive material consuming in its extraction large amounts of electricity. Glass and ceramics on the other hand involve little more than melting heat and are not highly endothermic. It should be possible to provide silicate-based materials with a much wider range of properties—mechanical, thermal and electrical—than

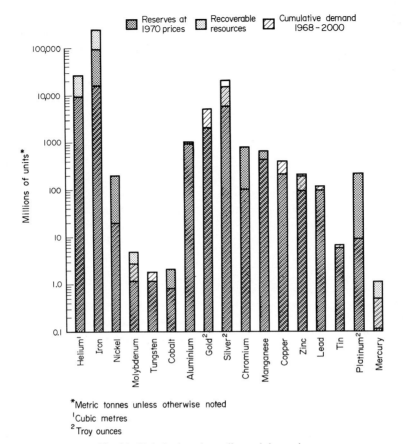

Fig. 16. Global mineral supplies and demands.

those of today. Table 14 gives the energy intensity of various materials.

Military Consumption of Resources

The problems of disarmament with its consequences for peace and world harmony are beyond the scope of this report which is not dealing with the ominous problems of conflict. Nevertheless, it is not possible to ignore the vast consumption of resources—scientific, manpower, materials and energy—which are consumed by the continuing race not only in arms but in the sophisticated effectiveness of military technology.

In the situation we have described, the gigantic waste through military preparations caused by man's distrust of man seems particularly tragic, and one must question the extent to which its elimination would give our race sufficient time to solve the global problems and create a stable world. Even a modest reduction of armament might buy the few vital decades which might make this possible.

At 1970 prices and exchange rates, the total world military expenditure for 1974 was estimated at $210.3 billion, an increase in constant prices of 68% on the previous 20 years. In 1973 at current prices the world cost was $244.4 billion, meaning that in every hour of that year

TABLE 14
Energy Intensity of Various Materials

Product	Energy requirement (MJ/kg)
Asphalt	6
Lumber	6-7
Cement	8
Glass	17
Iron and steel	24-42
Petroleum-based plastics	45-135
Zinc	65
Chromium	60-125
Aluminium	200
Magnesium	350
Titanium	400

Note: Ores and processes appear as of early 1970s. Savings possible in plant materials by using associated scrap as an energy source has not been counted. Chemical energy embodied in feedstocks is an additional 40 megajoules per kilogram for petroleum products and 16 megajoules per kilogram for wood products.
Source: E. T. Hayes, Energy implications of materials processing; E. C. John and S. B. Preston, Timber: More effective utilization.

the nations of the world spent $30 million on armaments and armed forces. In 1978, the military expenditures passed $400 billion although by far the greatest expenditure was on the part of the major military powers, some of the poor countries spend a high proportion of their total resources on this unproductive activity, while the arms trade drains away considerable sums from the poor to the rich. In contrast, aid given by the donor countries to those of the Third World amount to only around 4% of the military expenditure of the former. The build-up of armaments and increases in the size of the manpower developed for defence purposes in many Third World countries is often attributed to the success of the armaments trade of the developed countries. While this is no doubt an important element, it is by no means the full story. Many developing countries, through a sense of political and military insecurity, are in fact spending a very large part of the national budget and manpower for defence purposes and are bidding for advanced military equipment from the nations which have developed and manufactured it. Hence, this problem must be seen essentially in terms of regional tensions and geopolitics.

The resource implications of military expenditure are enormous. Nearly half-a-million scientists and engineers are employed in military research and development—almost half the world's scientific manpower—at a cost of almost $25 billion annually. This represents perhaps 40% of the total research and development expenditure of the world, public, industrial, and academic. The increasingly sophisticated nature of military technology means that the trend is likely to continue upward.

Behind all this is an enormous consumption of scarce raw materials and of energy in the form of petroleum products, explosives and the monstrous arsenal of nuclear weapons.

It would be naive to imagine that if, by a miracle, world disarmament were achieved, these resources would immediately become available for peaceful development; nevertheless, release of man's minds from fear and hatred of their neighbours would release a torrent of constructive possibilities which would enable many other problems to be solved.

Meanwhile disarmament negotiations drag along with little tangible result other than generation of frustration. It is extremely important that the disarmament negotiations should lead to constructive steps for freezing and then gradually reducing military expenditure. Politically realistic and practical mechanisms must be devised for channelling military expenditure towards productive goals, especially those of meeting the survival needs of all people of the world. A specially difficult problem to solve is the effects of disarmament on employment. The United Nations may call a conference specially dedicated to the relations between armaments and development.

CHAPTER **5**

Environment and Climate

Against the cosmic range of the forces and conditions of nature, man lives precariously within a thin and tenuous mantle of air, water and soil, adhering to the surface of the earth—the biosphere. This thin shell of organic existence, with a narrow range of temperature, enjoying a constant oxygen supply and buffered from excessive radiation from space by a layer of ozone, is warmed continuously by the sun, while vast accumulations of the solar energy of past aeons have accumulated as deposits of oil and coal. Within this equable biosphere man lives in symbiotic relationship with all other forms of organic life. Hitherto man has never seriously tested the fragility of his life system, although he has often suffered disasters to his environment, short-lived or lasting for centuries, due to external forces—volcanoes and floods, the advance or retreat of deserts, ice ages, earthquakes and the invasion of other organisms as plagues. Now, however, with the enormous increase in the scale of human activity, man's own actions appear to have begun to disturb the equilibrium of the planet. Within the biosphere itself, there are, of course, innumerable chemical substances, created, used or excreted by organisms and microorganisms which nature, over the ages, has accommodated into her equilibrium. Now, however, through his mastery of molecular architecture, man has created a myriad of new compounds, hitherto unknown in nature, many of which, after use or degradation, he discharges into the atmosphere, the soil, the rivers and the oceans. Some of these appear to be virtually non-biodegradable and are distributed unchanged throughout the biosphere or the upper atmosphere. We simply do not know as yet the capacity of nature to absorb these accretions, nor can we foresee their ultimate consequences. Such changes in the proportion of the natural components of the biosphere, or the addition of foreign material to it, is what we mean by pollution.

But pollution is concerned not only with the injection of man-made materials into the biosphere; it can also result from human intervention in the energy system. Above earth and water is the atmosphere which not only shields us from short-wave and other dangerous radiations, but through the "greenhouse effect" of the carbon dioxide component of the air, re-radiates energy and prevents the reflection of the longer waves back into space. Within the entire atmosphere and in intimate relation with the oceans, the hydrological system operates, where gigantic forces gather and disperse, move and consolidate to produce the world climate which we enjoy and suffer and know so little about. Although the energy involved in climatic phenomena is enormous, the balance is often precarious and can be upset by relatively small forces. We are thus equally ignorant as to the extent which our toying with energy, including the heat and carbon dioxide effluents of industry, quite small in relation to the forces of the atmosphere, can influence the system as a whole.

Pollution is, of course, no new phenomenon. Man has always tended to "foul his nest", and it is probable that bad agricultural practices in ancient times have turned much good agricultural land into desert. The "slash and burn" techniques of primitive agriculture were always environmentally undesirable. What is new and menacing today is the effect of the great increase in total human activity.

The basic problem of the environment is, then, the pressure of growth of all sorts, of population numbers, of activity and consumption *per capita,* of cities with the difficulty of removing human, industrial and solid waste, of the population of automobiles emitting carbon and nitrogen oxides, and in general the growth in the consumption of materials and energy in the industrialized societies. The fear is, that as a result of these increases and of the side-effects of uncontrolled technology on which contemporary society is built, we are pumping so much and so many waste substances into the air, earth and water, that we may be on the road to serious ecological disaster. Admittedly such pollution effects have been noticeable for more than a century and, indeed, during the earlier phases of the Industrial Revolution and into this century, industrialization was much more exploitative of nature and of man than it is today. The "dark satanic mills" of Victorian England, the sulphurous fogs, dirty rivers and adulteration of food, were much worse than today and were created with an irresponsibility and ignorance, which blissfully ignored the niceties of ecological balance. But these manifestations were localized in relatively few places in a few countries and hardly presented a serious threat to the ecosystem as a whole. The encouraging aspect of today's situation is, of course, that there is a general awareness of the ecological danger, much analysis of the problems and many new control and prevention measures to contain it.

It is not possible here to catalogue the numerous contemporary threats to the environment, and it must suffice to outline a few and to insist on the need for a much deeper understanding of the causes and consequences, pointing out some of the more serious and general effects which are also the least understood. It must also be stated that there is a great need to approach the broad problem of the environment with a mature sense of proportion. Some of the dangers are potentially extremely serious, others are relatively trivial and easily remedied. An unbalanced or fanatical approach can only serve to confuse the trivial with the vital and put a brake on much development important for other great human needs.

MAIN TYPES OF ENVIRONMENTAL PROBLEMS

We shall discuss briefly three types of environmental problems.

Firstly, there is that of the pollution of the air and water by short-life or biodegradable products of agricultural or industrial activity or consumerism. Most of the environmental action of the past decade has concerned pollution of this type, just because it is here that the danger signals have been most visible. To a great extent, as in the cases of carbon monoxide from automobile exhausts, sulphur dioxide from oil or coal combustion in factories, power stations and refineries, contamination of rivers by detergents, or the eutrophication of lakes through agricultural and industrial effluents, these ills have been allowed to develop as a result of insufficient appreciation of ecological considerations, insufficiently regulated by public controls and based on development decisions of a purely economic cost/benefit type which have ignored the indirect costs to individuals and the community. Industry has itself been taken by surprise, by the appearance of so many, so visible and so unwanted side-effects of its technological developments and still more by the public's reaction to their visibility. Most difficulties of this type can be eliminated or at least contained within tolerable limits, at considerable cost, it is true, but one which is bearable and probably less than that of the advertising outlay of the sectors concerned. Furthermore, it is easier and cheaper, in erecting new plants, to eliminate much of the pollution at the outset, than it is to clean up existing processes, so that a new generation of industrialization should be much cleaner than the present.

Already much progress has been made. London's "pea-soup" fogs are now only a memory; fish have returned to the Thames; Pittsburgh has been cleaned up. Much more remains to be done, however, as, for example, in eradicating smog of the Los Angeles type which, resulting from high concentrations of automobile emissions in difficult topological and climatic conditions, represents a dispersed cause, more difficult to tackle.

Air and water pollution are inevitably international and have no respect for national frontiers. Acid rain on Stockholm coming from the Ruhr or East Germany; sooty snow in Norway originating from the factory chimneys of the English Midlands; pollution in the Netherlands as the River Rhine pours into the sea the chemical effluents of Switzerland, France and Germany—these are obvious examples of the gradual diffusion throughout the ecosphere of the waste products of our mounting production (see Fig. 17). This transfer of pollution from one country to another is sufficient reason for attempting to harmonize national standards, tolerance levels and penalties. It probably justifies also the principle that the "polluter

pays". There is also need to harmonize the environmental regulations and standards of the different countries, if the industries of those countries with strict regulations are not to be penalized in international competition against those with more lax regulations. Many countries of the Third World, encouraging a rapid industrialization are also on guard against the preferential export of the dirtier industries of the pollution-conscious nations to the north.

Rather different considerations arise with regard to *the second type of pollutant,* about whose action, distribution and persistence in the environment, not enough is known. Examples of such chemicals or persistence, not easily biodegradable, are chlorinated hydrocarbons such as DDT, polychlorinated biphenyls, some phosphorous compounds, mercury derivatives and radioactive wastes. Much more research is needed concerning the life-span of such chemicals in the environment, how they are dispersed in nature, and their ultimate fate, as well as their synergistic effects and biological reactions.

In addition to problems of detection, toxicity determination and control, many difficult problems arise here, as in other environmental issues, which border on the topic of conflict of interest between different sectoral policies and goals, already referred to. Resolution of such problems involves a complicated cost/benefit analysis, using the words "cost" and "benefit" in the widest possible sense and involving moral considerations. A simple example from the first category above is whether, in a time of acute energy shortage where its conservation is a national objective, it is possible to continue to tighten standards of clean exhaust emission (which is another goal) as this may entail greater consumption of gasoline. Another example is furnished by DDT. When this chemical was first introduced during World War II, its general toxicological features were already known, and its application was decided upon, in the light of such knowledge. The relief

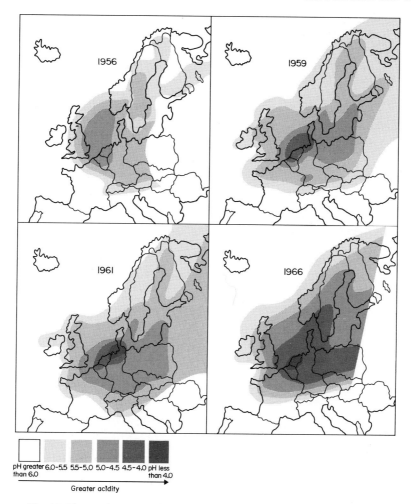

pH greater 6.0-5.5 5.5-5.0 5.0-4.5 4.5-4.0 pH less
than 6.0   than 4.0

Greater acidity

Fig. 17. The steady spread of acid rain in northern Europe from 1956 to 1966 is shown in this sequence of maps. The region of greatest acidity, around Belgium and the Netherlands, reflects both heavy emissions of oxides of sulphur and nitrogen and prevalent meteorological conditions in the region. (From S. Oden, Nederbordens forsurning-ett generellt hot mot ekosystemen. In I. Mysterud, ed., *Forurensning og biologisk milijovern,* Univeritetsforlaget, Oslo, 1971, pp. 63-98.)

it provided from the insect-borne diseases of malaria and typhus, which had caused such havoc in practically all previous wars was dramatically successful, while since that time it has relieved millions from the scourge of malaria and enabled them to lead tolerable and vigorous lives—incidentally contributing to the population increase. Nevertheless there are fears, based on considerable justification, that this particularly persistent chemical might, with widespread and indiscriminate use, in the end prove disastrous to the environment, despite the fact that there is, as yet, little evidence that it has caused any real damage to human life. It has already dispersed throughout the world, having been detected even in penguins' eggs in

TABLE 15

Chlorinated Hydrocarbon Pesticides in Human Adipose Tissue, US, FY 1970-1974*

Pesticide	Concentration in lipid (arithmetic mean, ppm)				
	FY 1970	FY 1971	FY 1972	FY 1973	FY 1974
Total DDT equivalent	11.65	11.55	9.91	8.91	7.83
HCB (benzene hexachloride)	0.60	0.48	0.40	0.37	0.32
Dieldrin	0.27	0.29	0.24	0.24	0.20
Heptachlor epoxide	0.17	0.12	0.12	0.12	0.10
Oxychlordane*	—	—	0.15	0.15	0.15
Sample size	1412	1612	1916	1092	898

*First full year in which oxychlordane was analysed was FY 1972 (FY = fiscal year).
Source: US Environmental Protection Agency, 1974.

TABLE 16

Persistence of Insecticides in Soils

Insecticide	Years since treatment	Per-cent remaining
Aldrin	14	40
Chlordane	14	40
Endrin	14	41
Heptachlor	14	16
Dilan	14	23
Isodrin	14	15
Benzene hexachloride	14	10
Toxaphene	14	45
Dieldrin	15	31
DDT	17	39

Source: R. G. Nash and E. H. Woolson, Persistence of chlorinated hydrocarbon insecticides in soils. Copyright 1967 by the American Association for the Advancement of Science.

Antarctica; it enters into the food chain of bovines and, through milk, into the human organism. It is also said to threaten some rare species with extinction, and there is a fear that it could, by ingestion by microfauna and microflora, eventually remove all life from the sea. Once again, there is insufficient knowledge to assess how serious such fears are, and again also we are here facing a situation of such complexity and involving so many of the cycles of nature, that it may never be possible to be quite sure. (See Tables 15 and 16.)

The final category of environmental threat is that of the quite general, global effects which might, if allowed to evolve in accordance with present trends, cause irreversible changes in the world climate and, in the extreme, imperil all life on earth. Here we enter a still darker zone of ignorance.

One of the mechanisms in question is that of

heat pollution of the environment, due to the heat released into the rivers and atmosphere as a by-product of the generation and use of energy by man in ever greater quantities. Such pollution will certainly increase rapidly as population rises and the standard of living improves—at least with present life-styles. Initial concern with regard to thermal pollution centered on the problem of the heating up of natural bodies of water by the discharge of waste heat from the thermal generation of electric power or from industrial processes such as steelmaking. The effect of such discharges varies greatly from site to site according to the natural features which control the mixing of hot water with cold and its eventual dissipation, and it is obviously more marked in general in river than in ocean discharge. The main danger is of considerable modification of the natural aquatic environment by the reduction of the oxygen content of the water, which also lessens the capacity of organisms in the water to detoxify chemical wastes. Such effects, although mainly of local significance, increase as electricity demand grows and is extremely important with regard to the siting of power stations in the future. It is doubtful that the rivers will have sufficient thermal carrying capacity to cope with the proliferation of power and particularly of nuclear power stations as demand grows. One proposed solution is to group colonies of nuclear generators on islands, natural or artificial, which would have the double advantage of using the great heat sink of the ocean for cooling and of removing nuclear danger from the vicinity of population concentrations. Even with such a system, one would have to expect ecological disturbance. (Fig. 18 presents the man-made power densities and areas. Table 17 gives the climate-related alterations associated with agriculture.)

More important is the problem of the total heating up of the atmosphere and of the earth's surface as energy use grows, with its possibly irreversible influence on world climate. It is not known with certainty how much general increase in the temperature of the surface and the atmosphere could be tolerated without dramatic changes in climate. It has been calculated* that a world population of 6 billion people, using energy at the rate *per capita* of Sweden in 1975, would contribute about 0.4% to the natural radiation balance of the continents, while estimates on the basis of a 20 billion population, using 20 thermal kilowatts per person would reach 2.6% of the radiation balance. Taking into account some of the more important of the phenomena of the atmosphere, this latter situation might give rise to a general temperature increase of 1.2-2.5°. The complexity of the global system of energy and climate is such that these rather simple calculations can only be regarded as rough indicators, but it does seem that thermal barriers do exist to long-term energy growth, although they may still be distant.

While the *general heating effects* likely to arise from the expected energy consumption of the early years of the next century are almost certainly within the limits of tolerance, it has to be realized that heat inputs are very unevenly distributed over the surface of the earth and not uniformly as existing models assume. It seems likely that a further one or two doublings of energy consumption would result in the heat level at a number of the world's most industrialized regions and would influence climate over many millions of square kilometres—perhaps another argument for a larger proportion of the world's industry being distributed throughout the Third World.

One matter that must be borne in mind in all discussions of geothermal pollution is that a large proportion of the water of the planet is locked up in the form of ice in the polar regions. Relatively small changes in temperature, by melting a proportion of ice, or

*A. M. Weinberg and P. Hammond, Limits to the use of energy, *American Scientist* **58**, 412 (July/August) 1970.

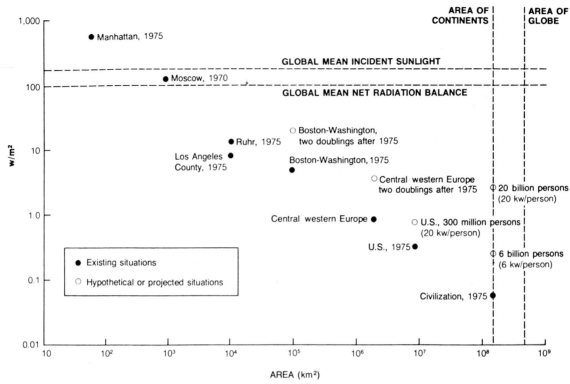

Fig. 18. Man-made power densities and area. Ten per cent of the net radiation balance has been reached over areas of 10,000 square kilometres and 1% over areas exceeding 1,000,000 square kilometres. (After National Center for Atmospheric Research, *Atmospheric implications of energy alternatives.*)

TABLE 17
Scale of Climate-related Alterations Associated with Agriculture
(around 1970)

Alteration	Magnitude
Conversion of forest to fields and grassland	18 to 20% of area of continents (albedo changed from 0.12-0.18 to 0.20)
Subsequent conversion of fields and grassland to desert	5% of area of continents (albedo changed from 0.20 to 0.28)
Area under irrigation	1.5% of area of continents
Reduction of continental runoff by irrigation	5%
Increase in continental evaporation due to irrigation	2%
Increase in evaporation from irrigated areas	100 to 1000%
Area covered by artificial reservoirs	0.2% of area of continents

Source: Study of Man's Impact on Climate, *Inadvertent climate modification.*

freezing still more, can have runaway effects on the climate to say nothing of potential and quite large changes in the level of the oceans.

In addition to the direct heating-up consequences of increasing human activity is the problem, already touched on, arising from the accumulation in the atmosphere of increasing quantities of carbon dioxide (CO_2) from the combustion of fossil fuels: Fig. 19 below. This space. Human activities appear already to have raised the carbon dioxide content of the air by some 10%, and it is estimated that by the end of the century, this will have reached 25%. This is estimated to lead to a warming up of the earth's surface by about 1°C on the average, with a bigger effect at high latitudes. This might well reduce the ice masses at the poles sufficiently to raise the level of the oceans and cause climatic

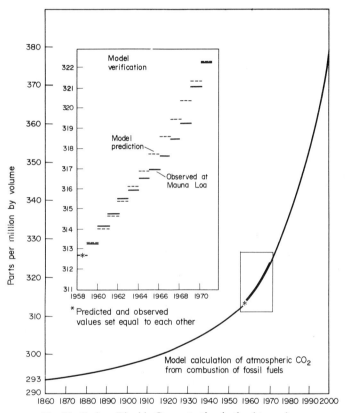

Fig. 19. Carbon Dioxide Concentration in the Atmosphere

gas, although occurring in the atmosphere only as a very small proportion, is vital to life on earth; it provides the nourishment of the plants which convert it by photosynthesis to sugars and starch. It is also crucial in determining the earth's temperature because, through the so-called greenhouse effect, it traps some of the earth's heat, preventing it from dissipating into disturbance at all latitudes. It must be mentioned once more that the carbon dioxide situation is much more complicated than its mere accumulation would indicate. There is, for example, the question of the solubility of the gas in the oceans and its liberation from aqueous solution with rising temperature. Also variations in the size of the planetary biomass, for example by the cutting down of tropical forests, could influence the proportion biologically absorbed. Some of these factors might increase and others decrease the proportion of carbon dioxide, and we are thus faced once more with great uncertainties. However, we must conclude that the carbon dioxide problem is a serious one and will have to be taken into account in long-term energy strategies, probably before all the factors are fully understood—an interesting example of the need for a new art, the management of uncertainty.

Under the auspices of IFIAS and other organizations a new project will shortly be launched which will study the "Consequences of a Hypothetical World Climate Scenario Based on an Assumed Global Warming due to Increased Carbon Dioxide".*

A further phenomenon, relevant to the subject of climatic change, is the existence of particles of carbon and other substances in the upper atmosphere, which absorb radiations and might be expected to lead to surface cooling—but even this is not quite certain. Much of this particulate phenomenon arises from natural causes such as forest fires and volcanic eruptions. Indeed it has been noticed that exceptionally cold periods often follow major eruptions. However, much of the particulate density results from human activity. On the other hand a heating-up effect does arise as a result of the deposition of carbon particles from combustion, on Arctic snow and ice, reinforced, perhaps, by oil-spill drifts, trapping solar heat by black-body absorption.

Considerable prominence has been given of late to the possible influence of certain chemicals in the atmosphere on the ozone layer of the upper air some 15-40 kilometres above the surface of the earth. Ozone, O_3, an allotropic modification of oxygen, O_2, is produced by the action of ultraviolet radiation

from the sun, on normal oxygen molecules. It exists to the extent of only about 15 parts per million in the stratosphere, but this is sufficient to provide a shield to the earth's surface against the penetration of ultraviolet radiation, damaging to plants and animals. It seems that life on earth did not appear until the ozone layer had formed. The pool of ozone in the stratosphere is maintained by a dynamic equilibrium of the formation and destruction of ozone from normal oxygen in ultraviolet light. A further influence of the ozone layer, through the heat generated by ultraviolet absorption, is to suppress the mixing of lower atmosphere air with that of the stratosphere, one of the element of climatic stability.

Destruction of the ozone layer is increased by catalytic action in the presence of certain chemical species, notably the hydroxyl ion from water vapour, nitric oxide and atomic chlorine. A 5% decrease in the ozone concentration involves a 10% increase in the radiation reaching the earth, and it has been stated that such an increase would result in an additional 20,000 to 60,000 cases of skin cancer per annum in the United States alone. This would probably not be the main danger, since the genetic material DNA and also proteins are particularly sensitive to radiations of this wavelength.

One of the potential enemies of the ozone layer is nitric oxide emitted directly into the atmosphere in the exhaust gases of high flying supersonic aircraft. This has been one of the main ecological objections to Concorde, but it would be much more serious from fleets of high-flying, heavy SSTs. A still more dangerous source of nitrogen oxides could be from the explosion of thermonuclear bombs, whose high temperature produces such compounds in abundance from the oxygen and nitrogen in the atmosphere. This might seem a trivial by-product of a nuclear war; this is not necessarily so, since depletion of the ozone layer could have a greater impact on non-combatant nations than radioactive fallout.

*Walter Orr Roberts, *Report from Symposium and Workshop,* Aspen, Colorado. 8-14 October 1978.

More recently, concern has moved to the effect on the ozone layer of the extensive use of aerosol sprays, now in common and increasing use for the dispersion of many products such as hair lacquers, deodorants, paint, insecticides and the like. The propellant is usually a chlorofluorocarbon, such as the freon compounds which are particularly inert and non-biodegradable and pass through the lower atmosphere unchanged chemically. There is therefore no natural "sink" for such compounds. When the molecules of such gases reach the stratosphere, however, there is evidence to show that they undergo photochemical decomposition by the ultraviolet radiation, releasing free chlorine which attacks the ozone by a chain reaction mechanism. The seriousness of this bizarre effect is difficult to assess, but there is evidence that it could be serious, especially since, if the uses of such substances were to be prohibited, the attack on the ozone would continue for a decade as existing molecules rise and spread.

Nuclear bombs, supersonic aircraft and even aerosol sprays are luxuries we could well afford to dispense with. Not so, however, is a further source of nitrogen oxides in the atmosphere, namely the generation of nitrous oxide by the anaerobic decay of agricultural wastes, the danger increasing with the quantities of nitrogenous fertilizers used. Evidence here is incomplete, and there may be a natural absorption of this gas or its oxidized product nitric oxide, before it reaches the stratosphere; if not, the phenomenon could mean biological disaster.

This grim list of possible calamities arising from the continual increase in human activities is everywhere shrouded in uncertainty. We simply do not know enough about the life of our planet, the dynamics of its equilibria or the interactions of the various mechanisms.

Many of the above issues are already the concern of the United Nations and of its Environmental Programme, There is need to sustain and increase such activity. The global problems being of enormous, but seemingly remote importance to all, seem to be the concern of none, since the individual nation states are each preoccupied with the problems of the moment. Thus, the United Nations has a special responsibility in this field, not merely to promote and carry out the necessary research on behalf of humanity as a whole, but working towards the design of a system of global management under uncertainty and in the meantime scanning the changing situation and making known the perils and their consequences.

CHAPTER **6**

Human Resources—
The Inner Limits

We have already mentioned the statement of the Club of Rome following the debate which centered on the report by Professor Meadows, *The Limits to Growth,* that the material limits, important as these are, are unlikely ever to be reached, for in front of them lie a whole series of obstacles of a political, economic, social and cultural nature and eventually, perhaps in the inherent nature of man.* It is the subject of this chapter not merely to begin discussion of some of these constraints, but to stress that the fundamental objective of development is improvement of the human condition, to provide for societies and individuals, the means to make possible a full and rich life: abolition of a degrading poverty, yes; but much, much more in the way of better health and nutrition, the enlarging influence of education, the possibilities of leisure and condition propitious for the self-development of each human being.

Such broad considerations involve deep philosophical and anthropological concerns, cultural and ideological values and traditions as well as the myriad interpretations which dif-

ferent people, from different cultures, give to the concept of the quality of life. To discuss these questions with the depth they deserve is far beyond the scope of this report, but it is essential to stress the need to recognize their fundamental importance and to outline some quality aspects which must be taken into account in planning development to meet the larger human needs.

Development, both in the industrialized and, alas, often in the Third World countries, is generally taken as being synonymous with *economic* development and too often in economic thinking the individual is a mere unit of statistics, while quality aspects are forgotten or ignored because it is difficult to quantify them. It is all too easy to consider development in terms of Gross National Product and to forget that it is for the benefit of mankind in a much larger sense. This is not to belittle the importance of economic development which provides the resources for social, cultural and other improvement, but merely to say that by itself it is insufficient. At low subsistence levels especially, economic development is an essential ingredient of a better quality of life.

*See also F. Hirsch, *Social Limits to Growth,* 1977.

74

POPULATION AND ITS DISTRIBUTION

Great differences of opinion exist as to what would be the optimum, stable population of the world. This is essentially a matter of balancing quantity and quality; it would be possible, obviously, to have a very large population living at a low material level, or a smaller population with better living conditions. In a world organized through independent sovereign states, each country has the right to determine its own population policy, but in the future this will have to be evolved in the light of the total planetary constraints. Different countries and environments have different needs as was indicated clearly at the United Nations Population Conference in Bucharest in 1974. Some countries, such as Brazil which are relatively empty and rich in resources have, understandably, a pro-natalist policy; they believe that national development requires a much larger population to give it substance and versatility. There is, also, a political tendency in many nations to feel that a larger population would increase power and influence.

On the other hand, some other countries recognize that severe restriction of population growth is necessary to preserve even their present levels of material well-being.

A few words should be said at this point on the subject of population *density*. It is popular in some quarters to compare the low population density per hectare, for example, of some of the African countries, with the much higher densities of some of the European nations and to infer, rather facilely, that the developing countries can accommodate several times more people than they now have. This is, as a generalization, fallacious, since population density is a very poor measure of over- or under-population. Shortages of many resources other than mere space—for example fresh water for humans and animals, fertile soil, suitable climate and possession or otherwise of important mineral deposits—make it difficult

to provide for even a sparse population in many areas. Large parts of Africa, North and South America and Australia are, or could quickly become, overpopulated in terms of the carrying capacity of the land. The European comparison is misleading in the longer-term view, because firstly that continent is blessed with very favourable soils and climate, and secondly the European countries are dependent on heavy imports of materials, energy and food. For example, Denmark, a major exporter of dairy products, eggs and meat, imported in the 1960s more protein than any other country on a *per capita* basis, equivalent to three times the average protein consumption of each Dane. Table 18 gives the population densities for different parts of the world during the period 1925-2075.

In view of impending constraints of food and energy, then, as well as of the infrastructural needs, it is necessary for all countries to reconsider their demographic policies, if indeed they already have such, or to evolve them if they do not already exist, in terms of the quality of life of their citizens some years hence. As part of this it may be useful for countries to make studies of the carrying capacities of their land in terms of productive soil, water availability and climate, to help them to assess what should be their optimum population. Such studies are essential to the evolution of realistic demographic policies. A few countries such as Australia and Canada* have already begun such work and the United Nations could assist in developing and making known the methodology for more general application. At the initiative of President Carter, a comprehensive study was recently carried out in the USA called Global 2000 which makes a careful analysis of the world situation in terms of Population, Environment and Resources.†

Population, Technology and Resources, Science Council of Canada, Report No. 25, July 1976
†*Global 2000*

TABLE 18
Land Area and Inhabitants per Square Kilometre, in the World and Major Areas, 1925-2075
(United Nations medium variant)

Major area	Land area (1,000 km^2)	Inhabitants/km^2						
		1925	1950	1975	2000	2025	2050	2075
WORLD TOTAL	139,450	14	18	29	46	65	80	88
NORTHERN GROUP								
(MOSTLY DCs)	60,574	20	23	33	42	48	51	51
US and Canada	21,515	6	8	11	14	15	16	16
Europe	4,931	69	79	96	110	118	120	120
USSR	22,402	7	8	11	14	16	18	18
East Asia	11,726	49	57	86	117	141	150	151
SOUTHERN GROUP								
(MOSTLY LDCs)	78,786	10	14	26	49	78	103	116
Latin America	20,535	5	8	16	30	47	59	63
Africa	30,227	5	7	13	28	49	70	83
South Asia	19,557	25	36	65	122	187	241	268
Oceania	8,557	1	2	3	4	5	6	6

Source: United Nations, *Concise report.*

There is much historical evidence to show that as standards of living rise, human fertility rates decline and hence there are many advocates of the thesis that the only way to ensure that world population growth decreases substantially is to achieve rapid economic growth. There is obviously much in this argument but great doubts exist as to whether general living standards could be raised sufficiently in time to prevent world calamities from the arising of huge, underfed populations. In the race between prosperity and population increase, the latter seems to be well in the lead.

We have already mentioned that the greater proportion of the expected increase in the world's population by the end of the century will be in many of the less developed regions. In some of the larger and more sophisticated countries in this category there are active programmes of family planning, some of which are beginning to result in a decline in fertility. No doubt many governments will adopt active policies to discourage population growth in the next few years. These may include various deterrents, physical and moral, but their effectiveness would depend essentially on the encouragement of family planning, placed in the context of social and economic improvement. The Bucharest Conference, despite its political overtones, has helped to "soften up" the situation to make this possible, but it is doubtful if there is as yet a sufficient sense of urgency.

Family planning and the campaigns of information and education to make it acceptable and effective are exceedingly important, and much technical improvement is to be expected in relation to the development of safer, simpler contraceptive devices which are acceptable also on local, religious, and cultural grounds. However, in many places, even where there is a rational understanding of its benefits and the need for it, its acceptance is seriously limited for deep-lying anthropological causes, difficult to eradicate. For example, in some cultures, it has been regarded as essential that a family should have a surviving son to support the parents in old age and for religious functions. In the past, in conditions of high infant mortality, and taking account of the appearance of female children also, this has meant a family of about seven. Although conditions have changed so that this is no longer necessary, the traditional urge towards large families persists. Some people argue that in such cases population growth cannot be expected to decrease without the introduction of old-age pension and other welfare schemes, but this again necessitates a prior improvement of the economy. There are of course many difficult ethical and religious problems raised by the necessity to control population increase, not the least of which is the conflict between the right of individual couples to have such children as they desire and that of society as a whole to restrict the numbers.

The industrialized countries, where fertility rates hover near, or below, the replacement level, will have their own, but different problems, if present trends persist. In the early years of the next century, the proportion of the world's population in the presently industrialized countries will have fallen below 20% of the world's total and may dip to 15% by 2050. Furthermore, the average person in these countries will be middle-aged, while that of some of the Third World countries will be not much over sixteen years old. It is impossible to envisage a world consisting of rich, elderly people well-fed and heavily armed with sophisticated weaponry, surrounded by the great majority of the world's inhabitants, poor, hungry, unemployed and extremely young. Such a situation could not persist for long, but even the shadow of its possibility should be sufficient to make possible the creation of some sort of New Economic Order, within which each nation would strive towards a self-reliance, but not a rigid self-sufficiency in a world of interdependence and mutual respect.

The fact remains that whatever progress is made by family planning and other mechanisms

of population control, world population will have doubled soon after the turn of the century. This will be especially serious in relation to employment, since the less developed countries will still have to absorb labour into agricultural activity in absolute terms, even though the relative share of labour in agriculture will decline. The burden on development programmes to incorporate labour into productive employment will be an immense task. In Fig. 20 and Table 19 are presented the conditions for a Zero Population Growth (ZPG) of the world as a whole. We see that a stationary world population may vary from 5.7 billions in the most favourable case to 15 billions in the worst case.

HEALTH ACTIVITIES IN THE THIRD WORLD

In recent years many diseases, hitherto scourges in the tropical countries in causing death or compelling multitudes to exist in bad health with consequent misery and lethargy, have been eradicated or diminished, thanks to improved measures of hygiene, the use of insecticides or the appearance of new drugs which can prevent or control specific maladies. This has, of course, encouraged the population explosion. Nevertheless, continuing low health levels exist for huge masses of the population and their alleviation is an important qualitative aspect of development.

In the developed countries, the provision of adequate health services has become an accepted part of life and is extensively subscribed by governments. In many developing countries, health care delivery services are rudimentary or non-existent. Frequently, the scarce health dollar is expended on a prestigious hospital building or elaborate pieces of X-ray equipment rather than on the preventative health programmes and basic primary care facilities which might bring the benefits of scientific medicine to the population at large. There is therefore an urgent need to perform interdisciplinary studies of a comparative nature aimed to devise more

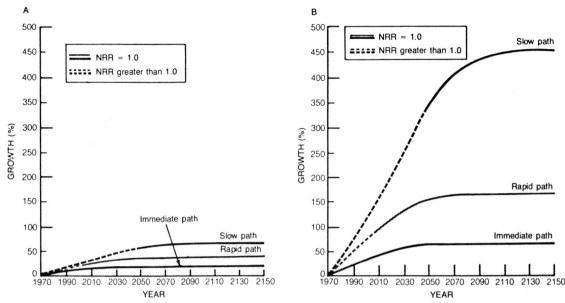

Fig. 20. A. Potential population growth in the developed regions by selected paths, 1970-2150. B. Potential population growth of the less developed regions by selected paths, 1970-2150. (Adapted from Frejka, 1973.)

TABLE 19
Three Paths to ZPG (Zero Population Growth)

	Year	Total population (billions)	Crude birth rate	Average annual growth rate	Average annual increment of population (millions)	Period	Net reproductive rate	Total fertility rate
Base population	1970	3.6	33	2.0	68	1965-1970	1.9	4.7
	If in year	The following characteristics are to be achieved				Then in period	The following rates are necessary	
Immediate path	2000	4.7	18	0.8	37	1970-1975	1.0	2.5
	2050	5.6	14	0.2	9	1980-1985	1.0	2.4
	2100	5.7	13	0.0	0	1990-1995	1.0	2.3
						2000-2005	1.0	2.2
Rapid path	2000	5.9	21	1.2	70	1970-1975	1.8	4.4.
	2050	8.2	14	0.3	21	1980-1985	1.6	3.7
	2100	8.4	13	0.0	0	1990-1995	1.3	2.9
						2000-2005	1.0	2.2
Slow path	2000	6.7	28	2.0	124	1970-1975	1.9	4.6
	2050	13.0	16	0.8	97	1980-1985	1.8	4.2
	2100	15.1	13	0.0	5	1990-1995	1.7	3.9
						2000-2005	1.6	3.5

Note: Changes required in demographic features in order to achieve the population levels projected in Figure 5-22 are set forth. Achievement of even the upper levels would require a significant decline in the 1970 total fertility rate.
Source: T. Frejka, *The prospects for a stationary world population.*

equalitarian and more cost-effective health care delivery systems structured to reflect the differing problems in the various developing countries.

Preventive medicine and effective therapy of disease depend on advances in medical science. Currently, the world-wide effort in medical research is quite large, being of the order of $5,000 million per year. However, a pitifully small proportion of these funds is going towards the creation of more effective measures to deal with the great health scourges of the Third World. In particular, tropical communicable diseases continue to take their devastating toll in terms both of mortality and morbidity. A high proportion of the people of the world suffer from the six most serious of these diseases, namely malaria, schistosomiasis, typhanosomiasis, filariasis, leprosy and leishmaniasis. The World Health Organization estimates that world research effort on tropical communicable diseases currently totals 30 million dollars, this miniscule proportion surely representing a change in world priorities. There is need for new measures, *e.g.* vaccines and better drugs, as the traditional measures such as vector control have clearly failed. Thus, a greatly expanded world-wide effort aimed at control of tropical communicable diseases is urgently required.

Health problems are closely associated with those of nutrition; and again inadequate nutrition, including that at the pre-natal stage, has an important although not fully understood relation to the general quality of development of the individual, for example his capacity to learn. Yet in many places nutritional levels are both quantitatively and qualitatively below those which indigenous foodstuffs, together with plants not yet used for food, could provide. Optimum possible nutrition in turn is often a matter of education, while the nutrition, especially of young children may possibly influence the capacity to learn and develop. IFIAS therefore, is considering launching a project which would take both nutrition, health and education into account for an optimal growth of the individual.

Health and hygiene have an important influence on many of the other problems we have discussed. For example the provision of clean and reliable supplies of drinking water, which are woefully lacking in many places, is essential to the improvement of health and the eradication of disease. Again, the existence of adequate medical facilities and of high levels of hygiene are probably essential for the success of family planning policies and hence an integral part of the population question.

While the above considerations apply to the basic problems of development in the Third World, problems of health and nutrition require serious attention in developed countries also. With affluence comes over-indulgence in eating, and especially over-consumption of protein carries a new series of health hazards. Changes in life-styles in the industrialized countries which may become necessary for total global needs would probably bring health benefits to the over-developed populations. Fig. 21 presents the major diseases in the poor countries. Much more financial and other resources must be spent on the eradication of the most serious tropical diseases, which may be the main debilitating handicap for self-help in the Third World countries.

An integrated view—nutrition, fresh water, housing, medical care and education—must be applied. More emphasis should be put on primary health care methods than on luxury hospitals.

EDUCATION

Education is an essential element with regard to facing up to all the difficulties and future needs we have discussed above. The many problems of education are well beyond the scope of the present work. Clearly the right to education is one of the basic human rights, but the question

Major diseases prevalent in poorer regions

Disease	Numbers affected	Disease	Numbers affected
Amboebiasis	Extensive	Plague	Fewer than 1500 cases per year(1960's)
Ascariasis (large roundworm infection)	Approx. 25% of world population	Schistosomiasis (Bilharzia)	Approx. 200 million
Bacillary Dysentery	Numbers of cases in the millions	Smallpox	65,000 cases (1972)
Cholera	Approx. 250,000 cases (1971-2)	Syphilis	Extensive
Endemic Typhus (louse-borne)	(1969) 25,000 cases	Trachoma	400 million (1960)
Filariasis	200 million	Trypanosomiasis and Leishmaniasis, and American Trypanosomiasis (Chagas disease)	Endemic in Central Africa at least 7-10 million in South America
Gonorrhea	65 million new cases a year (1964 est.)	Tuberculosis	15-20 million
Leprosy	11-12 million	Whooping cough	70 million cases a year
Hookworm disease	500 million		
Malaria	Approx. 100 million cases each year, 1 million deaths		
Measles	100 million cases each year		
Onchocerciasis	20 million		

Fig. 21. Data: G. W. Hunter, ed. *Tropical Medicine,* 5th Edition, W. B. Saunders Co., 1976; P. E. Sartwell, ed. *Preventive Medicine and Public Health* 10th Edition, Appleton-Century-Crofts 1973; J. S. McKenzie-Pollock, Planning A Healthier World, Unpublished manuscript; *Health Sector Policy Paper,* World Bank, March 1975; *1974 Report on the World Social Situation,* UN 1975; Fifth Report on the World Health Situation 1969-72, WHO, *World Health,* July 1976.

arises as to what kind of education, since it has to serve many purposes, the transmission of the accumulated knowledge of a culture to new generations, awareness of the world as it is, a capacity to learn throughout life, to say nothing of imparting immediately useful vocational skills.

Much effort has gone into the problem of abolishing illiteracy in less-developed countries, and this has only partly succeeded (Fig. 22). In many places where a basic educational system has taught the elements of reading and writing, a high proportion of the rural populations quickly forgets these arts through lack of opportunity to practise them—absence of books, newspapers and other material. Yet in some of these populations, technically illiterate, there can be considerable cultural maturity, with people well versed in local political affairs and the events of the world learnt over the radio.

It is now well established that education at all levels from unskilled workers to top management is an important factor in economic development, and accordingly much of the educational effort in many developing countries has economic objectives, although of

	Number of illiterates (in millions)			Illiterates as % of adult population		
	Male	Female	Total	Male	Female	Total
Developed[1] countries	9	18	27	2.4	4.3	3.5
Developing[2] countries	306	450	756	40.4	60.2	50.2
Total	315	468	763	28	40.3	34.2

1. All Europe, USSR, USA, Canada, Japan, Israel, Australia, New Zealand and South Africa.
2. All other countries excluding China, North Korea and North Vietnam.

Data: 1972 UNESCO Yearbook, p.47—48

Fig. 22. Adult Illiteracy (15 yrs. and older): 1970

course it has to serve cultural purposes at the same time; while this is probably essential, too much of it, especially at higher levels, has depended on the direct importation of education models from the industrialized countries and often from the former colonial power, often with little change in substance and curricula as well as structure. Often this has been introduced by countries exporting the models through a somewhat narrow conviction that theirs is the best system, which it may very well be for the home country; in other cases it can be a prolongation of cultural colonialism; much may be introduced which is extraneous to the needs of the receiving country and it can be irrelevant or even detrimental in the new cultural conditions.

Education in the developing countries, while of course it must contain many elements which are universal in their importance to individuals whatever may be their origins, should be evolved as far as possible in terms of the familiar environment, the history of traditions and the life-styles of local populations and in such a way as to widen their perceptions of the world.

Education is an integral part of the development process; people will not modify existing habits of thought, work methods, or nutritional and hygiene practices unless they understand

why this should be done and how they will benefit.

Education and its institutions are generally very traditional, derived from the function of transmitting the accumulated knowledge of the past and the cultural heritage to succeeding generations. Furthermore, teachers meritably teach what their teachers taught them. This conservative and conservationist approach has proved adequate in times of stability and slow change. Today, however, we are witnessing the transformation of the world and of society in a few short decades, and it would be a tragedy if the young were to be prepared, as is so often the case, for life in a world which is phasing out, rather than for a dynamic but uncertain future. There is need, therefore, for a new approach to education both formal and informal, an education which accepts and prepares for a changing world and which provides a capacity to adapt and to welcome the challenges of change. The education for the future is likely, therefore, to be considerably different from that of the present, less academic perhaps, but aiming, in addition to imparting the essential intellectual skills, at inculcating a capacity to learn and to adapt throughout life. For this we need to understand the learning process much better than now. The consequences of educational reform will probably be easily accepted by the flexibility of youth, but they will also have to be assimilated by those already adult, with an updating of the knowledge and information concerning the new conditions of living and the cultivation of adaptability by those in an age group which is biologically less flexible. Success in the implementation of development policies, in assimilation of new technology in hitherto non-industrialized regions, in creating indigenous and creative capacities for research and development, and many other essentials, will only be achieved if public understanding of the nature of the problems and the goals of the society is profound.

Enumeration of the educational issues is not appropriate here, but it should be stressed that there is great need for research on the learning process and on a better definition of the specific educational needs of different countries and cultures in facing up to the new conditions of life and work in our changing world.

CULTURAL INTEGRITY AND DIVERSITY

The development movement of recent decades, stemming as it does from the need to raise material standards of living in the Third World so as to make possible a more equitable distribution of wealth, has been dominantly economic in its nature and methods. The apparent economic success of the industrialized countries has suggested that their systematic pursuit of GNP increase through technology should serve as a model for the poor societies also. Furthermore, the privileged few in the developing countries, often educated abroad, have been attracted by this model and by the comfort, health and prosperity which it has brought them and which they see in contrast to local misery and hopelessness. In the process most of the agents of development have treated people as mere instruments of economic growth. Local cultures and traditional approaches have too seldom been treated with respect, but have been implicitly regarded as

mere barriers to progress. At the best, attempts have been made, for example in introducing new technological processes to adapt procedures to take account of what are regarded as social prejudices so that such developments should not arouse local antagonisms.

Thus, throughout this century there has been a gradual trend towards the spread of the material civilization of the West to become the basis of a monolithic world culture. True, many people in the Third World have benefited and equally true great improvements in material well-being are a fundamental need, but so far very little of the transfer of resources which the aid programmes have accomplished has reached the great masses of the people whose life in some cases has become actually impoverished in the process—as, for instance, through the migration of large numbers of country people to slum life and unemployment in teeming cities.

The elites of the Third World who have benefited most from aid of various types have in fact developed ambitions and appetites which are little different from those which are general in the rich countries. Often the result has been a cultural duality; acceptance of many of the western material values while retaining many of the original attributes of the local tradition, religion or way of life. Such duality tends to lead to conflicts, both within the individual and between different coteries of his society.

It is necessary to consider whether these are sound and healthy trends. There are strong arguments for encouraging and maintaining a diversity of cultures in the world and considering how development can be achieved in harmony with these and growing organically within each of them. A system of total uniformity throughout the world would be a poor substitute for the diversity of cultural systems which has existed in the past, each with its unique cluster of human values and its creativity.

A world constrained within a single pattern would be a spiritually poor world and its uniformity could probably be maintained only through controls and dictatorship. From a biological point of view also, diversity would appear to be invaluable in preserving the human capacity of adaptation to changing conditions.

The maintenance of cultural diversity would not mean a retreat into parochialism and mini-nationalism or the preservation of archaic and static social systems lacking a sense of global responsibility. What we envisage is the encouragement of a wide variety of evolving value systems and cultural patterns, interacting and reinforcing one another within a world of mutual interdependence. As far as development is concerned, respect for such a vision would demand an holistic approach which blended economic betterment with appreciation of human needs, social and spiritual as well as material.

IFIAS has a deep concern with this question of the value of cultural diversity, which was the subject of a workshop held in 1976 at the Villa Serbelloni in Bellagio.* Furthermore the Federation is at present preparing a project of immediate practical concern to the Islamic countries, which will consider the impact of technology on the culture of these nations and endeavour to establish guidelines to help in the selection of technologies appropriate to and assimilable within their traditions.

*Global Development: The End of Cultural Diversity?, IFIAS Statement from the Bellagio Workshop. *International Association* No. 8-9, 1976.

CHAPTER 7

The Political and Administrative Constraints

We have argued that the contemporary world is characterized by a growing interdependence of the nations, growing interaction between the major problem areas and the emergence of many problems of global dimensions which the individual countries cannot hope to solve in isolation. In the same way, the tangle of the world's social, economic, cultural, ideological and other difficulties can hardly be tackled today by the politician alone, by the economist in isolation, by the scientist or the engineer. This situation necessitates a concerted effort on the part of all of these and using contributions from all the scientific disciplines.

It is therefore extremely difficult for the existing institutions, both national and international, to take the transdisciplinary and plurisectoral measures that would seem to be indicated. On the national level, we are constrained by the myth of the eternal and sacrosanct nature of sovereignty, despite the fact that there is a progressive *de facto* loss of national power to act independently in many matters. The nation state projects the selfishness of the human individual into the collective attitude of chauvinism and also enlarges the importance of power considerations, making it difficult to look at the world problems in their totality.

The nation state, which is a relatively late arrival in history has had a major influence on the size and nature of the wars of the last century, by increasing the size of the units engaged, enhancing and focussing the poles of power and inducing global polarizations. "Sovereignty", says Toynbee, "is the cult of modern society and its gods demand blood sacrifice." Yet the sovereign nation state is likely to persist, although its powers may be eroded by regional arrangements and those necessitated by the nature of the global problems.

New means will have to be found both within and between nations, to tackle the new problems of change, complexity, uncertainty and scale.

One of the obstacles to attack on the global problems is the present stress on the purely political. Through the media and by other channels, the people at large are conditioned to think that political forces alone determine the pace and direction of change and to regard alternative options essentially in terms of alternative ideologies. This is not to detract from the reality and importance of the political function, but merely to stress the need to cultivate awareness that there are many other elements of growth and change which must be assimilated within the political process with the consent and understanding of the voter if wise decisions are to be made.

A further example of the contemporary approach to world difficulties is the domination of political decision-making by purely economic considerations. We have already stressed the need to take into account the social and cultural as well as economic costs and benefits and to attempt to quantify the externalities both at the national level and at that of the industrial corporation; in many countries it appears, at least from outside, that policy is often determined almost solely on criteria of short term financial expediency rather than on fundamental needs. While it is easy to understand this in times of economic difficulty such as the present, it is less clear why this should have been the case during a long period of economic growth.

It may be useful at this stage to look more closely at a few of the difficulties which face governments and international organizations in tackling the multiform elements of the *problématique*. The machinery of government was constructed for earlier, simpler times and has suffered little fundamental modification in recent decades, although it has greatly extended in size and scope. In general, government structures consist of a series of "vertical" ministries for sectors such as industry, agriculture, health, labour, education, foreign affairs, etc., together with central political, economic, and financial mechanisms. This rational system has worked well, on the whole, until now. But today so many of the problem areas are "horizontal" and sprawl untidily across the whole "vertical" edifice of government as we have seen so clearly demonstrated in relation to energy. Hence these problems tend to be tackled piecemeal, in terms of their impact, sector by sector. National policy often tends to be the sum of the sectional policies, not always completely harmonized, in the absence of an over-all integrated policy. In some countries, for example, responsibility for urban affairs is

diluted over a dozen or more departments and agencies. Attainment of the objectives of one departmental policy can easily give rise to difficulties in other areas of policy and the complex, intertwined nature of contemporary problems suggests that in the future we must increasingly expect intersectoral conflicts as well as unexpected interactions. This difficulty is, of course, recognized by many governments, and there are at present many experiments and improvements in intersectoral cooperation.

The over-all integration of policy is, of course, the function of the prime minister and his cabinet. However, these are so harassed by immediate and urgent political issues, especially in the parliamentary, democratic system, that they just do not have the time, or the detailed information necessary to deal with the extraordinarily wide range of interacting policy which contemporary government involves. The staff function (in contrast to the line function) found so necessary by large corporations and the military is rather weakly developed in national governmental structures and in international organizations is conspicuous by its absence. Furthermore when attempts are made to reinforce the staff function by the introduction of numbers of experts at the central, integrating level, this is often resented by the public as an apparent inflation of the bureaucracy, a dilution of democratic influence and a creeping technocratization. This was evident in the United States, with the great increase in the staff of the Executive Office. It must be admitted also that the strengthening of the central machinery is often feared by the sectoral departments and their ministers who see in the increasing importance of the staff function, a reduction of their power and independence.

The problem goes much deeper, however, than the top coordinating machinery since decisions have to be made at all levels and policy evolves throughout the hierarchy. Intersectoral impact is thus important in mini- as well as in macro-policy making. The traditional solution to this difficulty is the interdepartmental committee which is a useful, although often a heavy-handed and expensive device. It is also not uncommon for the interdepartmental committee to act as a meeting point of the representatives of the various departmental vested interests, in tacit agreement not to rock the boat by questioning each other's prerogatives or performance. Incremental changes are discussed and agreed, yes, but existing programmes tend to be sacrosanct. In the final analysis, coordination is usually effected by the Treasury, not always in possession of the facts or understanding of their significance.

A second difficulty arises from the conflict in political and administrative life, between short- and long-term concerns. The parliamentary cycle of three or four years between elections is a feature of all democratic governments and this means that both government and opposition parties have to respond rapidly to the issues which seem most immediate to the electorate. Governments, as individuals, tend to ignore problems which can be put off till tomorrow. In times of more leisurely change this probably mattered little, since the long-term problems were indeed far off in effect and importance. Today, however, with rapid rate of change as well as of rapid public perception of change, what could formerly be regarded quietly as long-term, tends to race into the period of five to ten years ahead, i.e. into the next administration. As a consequence, countries are tending to fall into a rhythm of crisis management, staggering from one emergency to another— monetary, social, balance of payments, unemployment, famines, student troubles, inflation and the rest—and then back to the next monetary crisis. At each crisis, we rush immediate remedial measures, which seldom reach to the roots of the fundamental issues of greater importance.

Of course, serious politicians and officials are well aware of these difficulties and the present interest throughout the world in studies of the future has given an impetus to the establishment of mechanisms endeavouring to explore trends and prepare for the longer-term situations. This is especially important with regard to military preparedness where it is necessary to attempt to foresee the technological and strategic thinking of potential enemies. Thus we have seen the arising of bodies such as the RAND and MITRE corporations in the United States. It is significant that these were created outside the official establishment, although working mainly on government contracts in order that bureaucratic rigidities and conditions of employment would not inhibit their work. There has also, of late, been a rash of "think tanks" concerned with economic and general civil problems, within or accessible to governments, which also work by contract and are also able to tackle problems for industrial firms under conditions of confidentiality. In Japan there are said to be some sixty of these. We have noticed at IFIAS that there is an increasing number of requests from private and governmental bodies and from the UN to help them with analysis and advice on complex issues which the bureaucracy cannot tackle.

The mystical allure of the approach to the end of a millennium has encouraged innumerable studies of what the situation of the world, of a country, or of knowledge in a particular subject, is likely to be in the year 2000, many of them not very impressive. It is, of course, impossible to foresee the future with any certainty and most of the techniques which attempt to do so are somewhat superficial. Nevertheless, in times such as the present, when we can no longer assume that tomorrow will be pretty well the same as today, it is important to probe the future, to examine the evolution of trends and to prepare alternative scenarios to have ready for use, should they be required. Projections such as the *Limits to Growth* prepared for the Club of Rome, for all their imperfections, are useful as a sort of prophylactic futurism. The authors of this study consistently stressed that their work was not that of prophecy, but an analysis of trends and their mutual impacts, so that policy changes might be suggested which would invalidate the projections.

Some governments have themselves created internal mechanisms for looking at the long-term future. For example, in Sweden, there is a futures secretariat attached to the prime minister's office, but serving the Swedish Parliament, which has survived two changes of the government in power and which gives regular advice on world and national trends. In France, the Ministry of Foreign Affairs has its prospective unit, responsible for preparing contingency scenarios to meet a series of possible international situations. More important than such useful but isolated innovations is the need to inculcate prospective thinking throughout the whole government structure. Similar offices are now being installed in many other countries.

A third and more delicate problem arises from the general public criticism of the bureaucracy, which is increasingly regarded as remote and unfeeling and behaving as an end in itself. No matter how intelligent and objective the civil service may be—and in many democratic countries this is uncontroversial—it is realized that its members are selected to provide stability and continuity as political administrations come and go. Hence the public service seems to stand for the maintenance of the *status quo,* to be the apotheosis of inertia and to resist change, especially radical change. There is some substance in these criticisms and it is very important that national administrations should be able and willing to attract people of innovative talents and to live with them. One of the major tasks of the administration in the future will be the management of change and complexity, and it must for this be capable of analysis of the alternative paths to national development, if its political masters are to be well served.

There are many other aspects of government structure and attitude which will have to be faced if the mysteries of the *problématique* are to be penetrated and dissipated. Here we can only mention the apparent paradox that, while the number of problems of a global character seems to be increasing and demands attention on the over-all scale, there is, at the same time, increasing demand for *de*-centralization, regional autonomy and participation of the individual in decisions which concern him. Ethnic and regional groups in many places are demanding autonomy—Basques, Bretons, Corsicans, the Welsh and the people of the Jura, to quote European examples only. If devolution of power in Great Britain gives a measure of independence to Scotland, the Shetland Islanders are beginning to consider asking for secession from Scotland. Actually the need for central and even universal consideration of certain problems and the apparently contrary trend towards a genuine devolution of power towards the province, the region, the district and finally the individual, are two sides of the same coin. The essential issue is how to establish in a harmonized manner, a system in which there may be many layers of decision-making in which the basic principle will be to ensure that in each issue, consideration and decision will take place as near as possible to those concerned, taking account of the intrinsic nature of the problems involved. Thus, for the global problems which in the end concern everyone, the decision will have to be at the global level; for local matters, at the town meeting. Many countries are already experimenting with provincial and regional devolution, but often in a somewhat rigid and legalistic manner. True devolution would require mobile mechanisms working in harmony to provide suitable interactions between the different levels. The corollary of devolution is participation—of workers in the management of their enterprises, of individual citizens in government. This subject is beyond the scope of the present work, but it must be pointed out that a trend to a more open and visible type of government is likely and that while this is in many aspects desirable it will pose difficult problems with regard to considerations involving security which, in the public interest, cannot always be open.

From our analysis of a few of the present inadequacies, the general conclusion is that there is great need to rethink the operation and the system of government, if we are to face up with confidence to the exigencies of the *problématique*. The need for innovation in the structures, procedures and attitudes of governments is clear, but the solutions are less evident, so that much institutional experimentation is called for. Essentially we require new mechanisms for the consideration of long term issues, for the identification and resolution of inter-goal conflicts and measures of decentralization and humanization of the administration. The achievement of this would necessitate a considerable deepening of public understanding of the problems and participation in their solution.

Of course, there are many current attempts to approach these problems. For example, the petroleum crisis led to the appointment of energy Czars and superministries, but some of these innovations turned out to be new forms of the old inadequacies—superministers unable to resolve intersectoral disputes and super-ministries encompassing several former departments, but preserving the partitions between them. Much more radical solutions are necessary.

The fundamental need is to create bodies of an essentially dynamic character of the transitory or temporary in contrast to the static structures and linear approaches of most of today's organizations. Organizations seldom try spontaneously to change procedures which are working or appear to be working well; methods are assumed to be optimum. In a benevolent environment alarm signals are rare and threats seem too remote to keep an organization alert

and free from complacency; lost opportunities are seldom even recognized; problems are tackled sequentially and errors arising from slightly inappropriate responses to slightly misunderstood challenges are brushed aside; difficulties are regarded as temporary setbacks rather than as resulting from basic trends. Yet, after decades of continuous economic growth, the environment seems to many to have changed from benevolent to hostile and the old tricks no longer seem to work.

The result is confusion. Organizations for the future, national and international, should be dynamic, adaptive, continuously self-renewing, participative, able to take risks and with inbuilt mechanisms of self-destruction to ensure that they disappear or have to be deliberately regenerated in new styles when their mission is achieved or if they show signs of senescence.

It is probable also that future institutions will be more pluralistic than those of today, with a less sharp distinction between the strictly official and the informal. There are already some examples of this, as in the Economic and the Science Councils of Canada, which although financed by the Federal Government, have been given a high degree of independence. They are thus in a position to criticize and comment on government policy, without party-political bias and, although their comments are not always welcomed by the establishment, they are thoroughly salutary.

On the international level, the organizations of today are mostly much more rigid and even more difficult to change than the national administrations and the case for their radical reform is generally admitted. However, with their authority shared by their member countries which, in the case of the United Nations, means practically all the nations of the world, change in depth is at present well nigh impossible in the absence of a universal political will to make them effective. Here again, recent years has seen the arising of informal bodies such as the Pugwash

Movement, the Club of Rome and Amnesty International, which, although not conceived as in opposition to the international establishment, are able to suggest, comment and criticize constructively, puncture complacency and induce greater public understanding of the problems. We are likely to see more developments of this kind.

Apart from change, the other major difficulty, arising from the new scale of today's activities, is that of complexity. The human brain is normally able to analyse the implications of only a few influences simultaneously and bogs down under the difficulties of weighing a large number of variables and uncertainties. The intuitive skill and experience of decision-makers, whether in politics or industry is no longer able to cope with the *problématique* situation as in the past. Choice of what seems to be the obvious way out of a problem often brings unpleasant responses—now termed counter-intuitive consequences. One of the new needs therefore is for better analysis of problems, the creation of alternative scenarios and the working out of the probable impact over a range of other policy areas. Decision-makers are instinctively suspicious of such a rational approach which involves the work of analysts and experts from many disciplines, as somehow representing a loss of authority. However, such experience as there is, indicates that if mutual confidence can grow up between the decider and the analysts and each respects the other's functions, such a partnership can be very enriching and still leave place for judgement, experience, the human qualities and the political component. More difficult perhaps is the technical problem of analysis of multi-national systems, availability of reliable data and certainty as to the assumptions. A great step forward has been made by the model of Mesarovič and Pestel,*

*M. Mesarovič and E. Pestel, *Mankind at the Turning Point,* Dutton, New York, 1974.

which although not yet a reliable decision-maker's tool, gives hope that the approach of investigating alternative strategies and policies is a real possibility for the future. Even now it can provide real insights to political leaders and can identify counter-intuitive mistakes before they are made. It is being tried out at present by several governments.

A few, final words must be added concerning the problems of uncertainty. Present forecasts with regard to many of the features of the economy or the direction of social change are widely divergent and vary from the hopelessly optimistic to the apocalyptic. This is well illustrated once again by the energy situation, where the scenarios with regard to the size of future oil reserves and the economic potentialities and social acceptability of other energy sources are brutally diverse and especially in relation to the uncertainties of non-traditional energy options owing to the technological problems, as yet unsolved and the extremely long lead time of research and development. Thus there are irreconcilable scenarios for future development which are, nevertheless, of major policy significance to countries and, indeed, also to the large corporations. These uncertainties are tending to force decisions to the top political level. In both government and industry much of the policy-making originates at a relatively low level in the hierarchy and evolves, is modified and refined as it reaches the decision-making point. With present uncertainties this is hardly possible, since the basic elements are often contradictory and the data unreliable; decision has therefore to be taken more often on the basis of political experience and intuition, with constant modification as new elements become available, with contingency approaches and plans ready, in case the original basic assumptions later appear to be wrong. A telling example is that of the possible influence of carbon dioxide on future world climate in relation to energy policy, for example in decisions concerning nuclear versus coal expansion plans. Here basic policy determinations may have to be made before the full facts are known.

One thing is certain: the new world into which we are passing will be very different from that of our fathers and its governance will be much more difficult. The challenge to the political system and to public administration is enormous. We know, as yet, little about the management of scale, complexity, change and uncertainty. But this is an art which will have to be cultivated—and quickly.

CHAPTER **8**

The Potentialities and Limitations of Science and Technology

This report, as is evident from its origin, is concerned largely with the influence which science and technology have had in shaping contemporary society and hence with the potentiality of these forces for the further beneficent development of humanity as a whole, as well as in pointing out some of the limitations and dangers which undirected scientific development might have. In this chapter we shall look more closely at some of these questions as well as at their policy implications for both industrialized and developing countries.

SCIENCE AND TECHNOLOGY IN INDUSTRIALIZED SOCIETIES—SCIENCE POLICY

Our present industrial societies and, indeed, a large part of the prosperity of the world, are built on a highly successful technology, originally based on mechanical ingenuity and invention but, increasingly, later derived from scientific research. The enormous growth of research and development resources since the end of the second world war has been spectacular and, although much of it has been for

defence, the economic growth has been strongly nourished by the products of such research. For individual countries in the industrialized world, economic success has come, not only from their indigenous research but also from products and processes imported from other countries, through purchase and exchange of patents and know-how and thus embodying the results of research done throughout the world. It appears, in fact, that for countries above a certain level of scientific effort and technological development experience, the diffusion of technology across national frontiers is sufficiently quick to compensate for inadequacies in their own research and development efforts. Japan is, of course, the archetype of a country which has relied with great success on imported technology. These conditions simply do not apply to the countries of the Third World. The level of research and development activity is too low to provide an awareness of world technological development to allow them to select with certainty from the wide range of new possibilities those particular processes and products best suited to their industrialization needs.

This concept of a threshold of scientific and technological activity and awareness below which the question of new technology or the accumulation of processes from abroad is quite fundamental in relation to transfer of technology. This is the basic reason why the construction of indigenous capacities in this field are essential to all countries hoping for speedy development.

By far the biggest proportion of research and development of the world is undertaken in the industrialized countries, although it is difficult to be sure to what extent their economic success is due to this and how much their high research intensity has arisen because they could afford it. Well over 90% of the world's research and development is in the industrialized part, possibly as much as 95%, so that the disparity between the rich and the poor countries in science is even greater than in income distribution.

In the developed countries, as we have seen, the appearance of unwanted side effects of technology has given rise to misgivings about the ultimate benefits of such development. To many, and especially to the young, life seems to be dominated by an inhuman technology, enforced by a faceless bureaucracy, so that the quality of life appears to be draining away, albeit the majority, despite their dislike of the side effects of technology, demand ever increasing material benefits from its working. Thus technology is on trial, and science, which has given birth to it, is under suspicion; it is at once the Cornucopia from which endless riches flow and Pandora's Box. Yet there is every reason to believe that scientific research has still an enormous potential for human betterment, both in the containing of pollution and other consequences of unwise, technological development, in creating a new industrial system which will better serve the needs of man, in abolishing the poverty of the masses of the poor, in exploring the outer limits and determining the extent and reality of the dangers which threaten the biosphere and in exploring the nature of man and his societies. More, rather than less, research is required, but there is need to reassess the place of science and technology in the workings of society so that they may better serve over-all human needs than in the past and help in the achievements of new objectives. If science is to serve humanity as a whole, and if its applications through technology are to be developed so as to ensure the maintenance of an environment suitable for human life, there will have to be a major reorientation of research programmes and attitudes in terms of priorities very different from the present. Amongst other things, applied research must no longer be conceived mainly as a problem solver to provide "fixes" when weakness in the economy appears: the scientific method will have to be applied in the holistic approach to the creation of new systems, technological, social, economic or ecological.

But let us look for a moment at the existing priorities of research and development, those fields of endeavour which have been the justification for the large increase of research resources by governments in recent years. So far, there have been three main objectives, namely defence, economic growth and national prestige. The latter includes items such as placing men on the moon, and the earlier "Atoms for Peace". The social and service sectors of the economy have attracted research resources of a lesser order of magnitude and we know even less about innovation in such activities than we do for technology. The social sciences are relatively poorly supported and, with the exception of economics, social science thinking has attracted only marginal attention from governments and industry.

What then of the future? Firstly, it has to be realized that there is much new technology in the pipeline. World research activity has, until recently, been rising steeply for several decades and, since the lead time from scientific discovery to the application of its results is long, the cumulative effect of this massive research effort should soon become visible in the form of important new technological developments with a major impact on industry, agriculture and society in general. Then there is the possibility of applying much new research from the world's accumulation of knowledge to the traditional sectors. Much of existing industry still operates on the basis of empirical inventions made long ago, gradually modified and improved on the basis of scientific discovery—new and more appropriate materials, better understanding of thermodynamic principles, and a multitude of significant minor innovations. Although effective and reliable, the older sectors are capable of still further improvement, for example in the form of new types of textile machinery, the use of electronic and other controls, further steps towards automation and many other approaches to greater efficiency, quality and precision. In particular, the potentialities for reduction of energy and materials consumption and in the elimination of pollution, are considerable. Many of the energy conversion processes are in this category. The internal combustion engine, for example, has remained virtually unchanged for decades, is of low efficiency, and depends essentially on gasoline as a fuel. Attempts to clean the exhaust emission results in still lower performance. Much remains to be done here, but the enormous mass-production success of the automobile industry has been encouraged by design improvement, the creation of fashions and other non-technological methods of maintaining and increasing sales, with little really innovative research.

Thirdly, as we have noted, most countries, including the most affluent, still have economic growth as an explicit national objective; this, of course, implies a still further development of technology, not merely of the types just mentioned which aim to increase manpower productivity, but also major innovations, new processes, new products, and new systems.

Beyond all this there are enormous potentialities for the uncovering of new knowledge and its application for the solution of the problems of humanity, the application of the "scientific method" to political and corporate decision-making and in the growth of the social sciences.

In view of the general circumstances described in this chapter, it will be necessary to ensure that the new technology will be socially acceptable and to avoid the augmentation of the difficulties which a too exclusive concentration on military and economic demands from earlier generations of technology has produced. This is why there is so much interest in the possibility of foreseeing the social and cultural, as well as the economic, consequences of various technological options. It is interesting that in the United States an Office of Technology Assessment has been set up by Congress for this purpose, rather than by the Executive Branch, to ensure that such matters are understood in sufficient detail by the legislators.

Even with lower rates of economic growth forced on the industrialized countries by higher labour costs or shortage and price increase of energy and materials, much research will have to be done, for example, on more efficient use of materials and fuels, recycling of metals, devising of products with longer lives and the reduction of pollution hazards. Again the need to evolve efficient, sophisticated but labour-intensive technologies for the Third World countries is a major challenge to industrial scientists, as is the corresponding desirability of evolving methods of manufacture in the industrialized countries which have a much higher work-satisfaction than the mass-production line arrangements of today.

The global problems likewise pose great and essential tasks for science. To avoid too close an approach to the limits of human expansion or survival, it is necessary to know much more about the workings of the planetary system, of the balance of forces which determine the stability of the climate and the atmosphere, of the nature and movements of the largely unexplored 70% of the earth's surface which is covered by the oceans and many other lines of enquiry which necessitate intensive and extensive research. So far insufficient attention has been given to these matters, but in the reorientation of world research they will have to be given high priority. As these matters are of common concern to all nations, there is great scope for a more serious attempt to develop international co-operation in research, through common programming between the nations and a division of the tasks and the costs between them.

To achieve the new research objectives, a great deal of rethinking of science policies will have to take place. There are also strong arguments in favour of the gradual construction of a global science policy. Hitherto national science policies have evolved, somewhat *ad hoc,* in response to immediate issues and in not too close a relation to economic, and still less to social, policies. The new science policies, if they are to respond to the real and permanent needs of society, will have to be conceived, not as autonomous areas of policy, but constructed carefully in intimate articulation with other policies and especially with social, economic, educational, health, external affairs and other sub-policy fields of the nations.

One aspect which is insufficiently appreciated by political decision-makers is the essentially long-term nature of the scientific process. In fact, the tempo of science is greatly different from the tempo of politics. From the first arising of a new concept in the mind of a scientist, through the fundamental and applied research stages and development to a significant extent of production, takes upwards of thirty years. Of course, this can be greatly shortened by crash programmes, but these are exceedingly costly and must remain the exception. Yet in the thinking of most economists, research and timely new technologies are con-

jured up as a result of the interaction of economic forces to be available when required. This implicit reliance on the "technological fix" can be dangerous in times of rapid change as at present. If the interval between two distinct sets of social and economic situations is shorter than the lead time of scientific and technological development, the results will come too late to contribute to essential problem solution. For this reason research on the great anticipated problems of the beginning of the next century should be started now. Of course, it is impossible to foresee the future with any precision and hence a number of options may have to be developed. Kenneth Boulding once stated that those who dare to predict the future are either astrologers or economists. This attitude is now obsolete: the inexorable changes in the world, force us to look ahead if we are to attempt intelligently to adapt in time to future difficulties. An individual who does not protect his family and society by insuring against uncertainty, as for instance when he drives on the roads, is regarded as irresponsible and in some cases criminal, yet governments do not insure against future uncertainty by exploring in advance against contingency. For instance, in the era of cheap oil, there was no incentive to industry to develop alternatives. Major programmes on the production of high calorific oils and gases from coal were abandoned a decade or more ago, because there appeared to be no urgency. In the future it may be necessary to develop many contingency processes to the pilot plant or prototype stage and also to assess, well in advance, the possible environmental effects of new developments. This will, of course, be costly, but much could be done again by international co-operation and cost sharing.

There is another trap in too great reliance on the "technological fix" approach, namely that the hurried construction of a technical solution to a major problem is seldom thought through sufficiently in social and human terms and can provide surprises in the form of new, unforeseen problems as grave as those which have been solved. There was something of this kind in the Aswan Dam scheme whose planners gave insufficient attention to agricultural and health consequences. Amongst other effects was an increase of the disease bilharzia, carried by water snails. A further, if minor, instance was cited at a recent meeting of IFIAS. A United States scheme for fuller utilization of the waters of the lower Colorado river resulted in a salting up of the water which flowed over the frontier into Mexico. By international agreement, the US government agreed to pay for a technological solution, namely the desalting of the water in Mexico. This new technology is expensive and energy consuming and may well cost more than the value of the practices which allow the salt to enter the water. Thus we have the tendency for "technological fix" to lead to still further "technological fixes". This warning against too exclusive reliance on the technological fix should not be taken to advocate that technological solutions to problems should be avoided, but merely that much deeper consideration of their tempo and consequences is needed than hitherto.

In the new research era, the need for transdisciplinary attack on many of the problems will be necessary. Much lip service is given to such an approach, but in practice the results are unimpressive. Both research and university structures tend to be unidisciplinary—as vertical as are those of government—and it often damages a scientist's promotion prospects to take part in transdisciplinary teams instead of writing papers on his own specialization. There is a positive need to encourage those who want to do inter-disciplinary work and to evaluate the quality of their performance in an inter-disciplinary context. New methods and structures will have to be found if the research of the future is to be soundly evolved within a social and economic framework. This is where IFIAS comes in; its constituent institutes represent a broad range of the disciplines and together they

can contribute significantly to attack on the global problems. Thus the scientific community has taken a first step in the new direction, but very much remains to be done and corresponding transformation of government policies is needed. IFIAS is actively involved by its members in a few programmes relating to the scanning and mobilization of the world's scientific and technological potential for attacking the global problems. Of special interest worth mentioning, is the project for Unesco's programme, "Research and Human Needs", called *Research trends and priorities in relation to Human needs problems.* Furthermore, IFIAS is presently carrying out a scanning amongst its member institutes of the status of the fields of natural sciences, social sciences and political sciences in relation to global problems. A first report on the nature of global problems susceptible to scientific attack was delivered by IFIAS to the UN Office of Science and Technology in 1978.

This stress on transdisciplinarity and on problem-oriented research does not, of course, mean that free choice, fundamental research on the whole spectrum of scientific disciplines, should be given less attention or be regarded as obsolete. The contrary is true; we badly need to deepen knowledge in many specialized fields, both for the basic cultural purpose of extending knowledge for its own sake and to add new pieces to the mosaic of understanding of man and his societies.

SCIENCE, TECHNOLOGY AND THE DEVELOPING COUNTRIES

The inadequate scientific and technological effort of the Third World requires special consideration. At the outset, however, we must stress once more that this group of nations is far from homogeneous and that the problems of research and development in India, for instance, with its highly developed and sophisticated system, or of the potentially rich and developed Brazil are very different from those of many countries in Asia, Africa and Latin America which possess very meagre resources in terms of scientific manpower, research budgets or laboratory facilities. We proceed therefore on generalities, with the understanding that each national case is unique and that policies for scientific and technological development must be designed specifically to meet the needs of each country.

We have already noted the fact that a quite overwhelming proportion of the world's research is done in the industrialized countries and that the existing scientific capacity of the developing countries is quite submarginal to their needs, including that of exploiting effectively the great accumulated store of world knowledge in science and technology, of selecting from it those elements appropriate for their own development, of modifying it for adaptation to the use of local raw materials and manpower possibilities as well as to the specific requirements of both domestic and possible export markets. The disparities in technological potential are, in fact, even greater than the over-all research statistics indicate, since it seems that the less developed a country is, the greater the proportion of its small research effort is devoted to fundamental research in contrast to applied research and technological development, an understandable situation since such countries often lack the industrial infrastructure to provide equipment and other facilities to carry promising possibilities in basic research through the applied research and development stage which costs, on the average, ten times that of the research on which it is based. The United States and the Soviet Union each possess about 18 engineers per thousand of the population, the European countries rather more than half of this, while in most of the countries of Asia and Africa, the number ranges from 1.3 per thousand, down to practically none. The reduction of these disparities

is an essential initial objective in creating adequate technological capacity.

Traditional methods to promote tertiary and quaternary education of scientists and engineers from developing countries have involved sending them to industrialized countries to acquire research skills. This has succeeded only to a limited extent, both because the training tends to be geared to technological standards of too great scale and complexity to be really relevant to the development needs of the student's home country and partly because of the "brain-drain" problem in which the cream is skimmed off for use in the already scientific rich countries. Another difficulty is that when such students return to their home countries, in the absence of sufficient technological structure, little use may be made of their newly acquired skills for national development needs and they continue to do fundamental research, considering themselves, as it were, expatriates of the world scientific community working in unfavourable conditions.

More recently there have been experiments which invert the process by bringing advanced research skills and personnel to the Third World countries so that the research and development proceeds in a realistic context. Notable examples are the International Centre for Insect Physiology and Ecology in Kenya, which is an IFIAS Member Institute, the International Laboratory for Research on Animal Diseases and the Research Training Centres of the World Health Organization and the International Institutes for Agricultural Research. These show much promise of producing really important results relevant to the world's needs and also have an important training function. We would like to urge more initiatives of this general character. An implication that deserves urgent attention is that such schemes can only be finally successful if there is a career structure in the developing countries for the researchers who will emerge from them. Therefore attempts must be made, amongst others by

IFIAS, to convince political leaders at many levels in the Third World so that these matters shall be incorporated at all stages of planning. Technological growth in the developing countries depends as we have said on the creation in each of a scientific competence; this can only come about if there is the political will to do so and this in turn has to be based on an understanding of the benefits of such an investment.

We return now to the question of the transfer of technology. When, in the decades following the end of the second world war, deliberate attempts began to be made on a significant scale to stimulate development in the Third World countries, it was recognized that technology was a key factor, whether in the production of food, the conquest of tropical diseases or in industrialization. It seemed obvious that the developing countries should make use of the vast accumulation of technology in the world and not have to repeat the laborious and costly process through which it had been elaborated elswhere. Transfer of technology was thus seen as an obvious and major tool of development. On the whole, however, transfer has proved to be more difficult than had been envisaged, and its results have been somewhat disappointing. The reasons for this are not fully appreciated, but it is increasingly recognized that they do not reside by any means entirely in technical considerations, but involve a number of quite fundamental questions concerning the nature of development itself. Hitherto, development policies have been based on a number of assumptions, of which the following are amongst the most important:

(1) Despite its shortcomings, the enormous success of the industrialized world in achieving material prosperity through the systematic pursuit of technology-based economic growth has been taken to indicate that this is the unique and inevitable path to be followed by all countries.

(2) It is assumed that the benefits of economic growth "trickle down" from the rich to the poor sufficiently quickly to ensure acceptable general development.

(3) It has been further assumed that technologies developed for a particular industrial, social and cultural environment can be transferred smoothly and advantageously to quite different environments.

These matters will, no doubt, be looked at differently by different people, both in the industrialized and in the developing world, but such assumptions should be questioned regularly. Nobody will deny that material growth is desperately needed in the Third World. For those near subsistence level, economic growth is the main hope for the alleviation of hunger, poverty and ill health. Beyond this minimum, the nature of development is less obvious and may be seen quite differently through the eyes of different cultures. Thus in the building up of the economy in societies of different traditions and circumstances, the technologies required to attain national objectives might well be different from those which have emerged in the presently industrialized societies in terms of a temperate or cold environment and the acceptance of the work ethic. IFIAS is at present at the beginning of a project to examine this question in relation to the cultural and social objectives of Islamic countries. Again, in quite other circumstances, demographic pressures may call for labour-intensive technologies which could well be quite sophisticated, but which are not likely to evolve in the industrialized North, where innovation will probably continue to be directed towards the increase of labour productivity and hence, high *per capita* employment of capital. Thus technology should be developed so as to be *appropriate* to the social and cultural needs of a country, in addition to being economically effective.

This concept of appropriate technology is, in fact, important for both developed and developing countries and if interpreted in its real meaning is far from being a euphemism for persuading the developing countries to adopt inferior technological processes and hence being reconciled to inferior economic levels. For developed countries the concept is just as important. Much of their technological development has aimed at achieving high levels of labour productivity and large scale production to provide for world markets and to take advantage of economy of scale. To this end it has been appropriate. Where it has deviated has been in its failure to take account of social and environmental factors: a polluting technology is an inappropriate technology, as are those which reduce satisfaction in work. Furthermore, as economic growth has increased, demand has often been stimulated for the acquisition of products which do little to meet real human needs, and thus Western technology seems now to be increasingly inappropriate in face of world difficulties. It is doubtful if these capital- and research-intensive industries with low labour intensity and their products are necessarily the ideal for the present needs of the masses of people in many Third World countries where different needs have to be met, not the least of which is to create employment.

This argument does not mean that countries at an early stage of technological development should reject Western technology. Much of it, including steel mills, oil refineries and fertilizer plants, is essential to provide the basis of industrial growth of all kinds. Furthermore, it is advantageous for such countries to have a proportion of its new industry of an advanced type, both to provide foreign currency through exports and to provide a basis of scientific, technological and managerial skills for future development. What is appropriate is to provide a mix of industrial approaches which will pro-

vide for mass human needs in the country, will provide employment and will assist in the upgrading of local manpower quality and skills to ensure a potentiality for later developments. The mix will vary from case to case in accordance with the availability of resources, skills, capital and social environment.

The second element in this mix is the creation of efficient, labour-intensive technologies, geared to local conditions. There is no reason to suppose that if the countries now heavily industrialized, instead of devoting their research and development to processes to increase productivity, had directed their efforts to the creation of labour-intensive technologies, they would not have been equally successful and they might, incidentally, have provided a much higher degree of work satisfaction. Such technologies should not have any status inferiority as compared with the often inappropriate, capital-intensive technologies and would, in developing countries, often be of small scale and thus suitable for decentralization, relieving urban pressure and bringing wealth to rural areas.

In evolving national policies for science and technology in many developing countries, special attention is needed with regard to a possible third element in the technological mix, namely the application of simple scientific principles to the improvement of tools and methods in the traditional sectors which involve the overwhelming masses of population, so far virtually untouched by technical improvement. So far most attempts to improve the lot of the rural populations have been to replace age-old traditional methods and tools by imported technology, such as farm mechanization, with uncertain success and often with social resistance and inefficient operations, since the new methods are not always seen as conforming to local needs and cultural habits. Furthermore, such replacement often results in decreased employment and migration to the cities. Much could be done by the application of well understood and often simple scientific principles to the improvement of traditional tools with a minimum of cultural disturbance.

The whole question of technology transfer is under discussion in many places and especially at UNCTAD; it was a main theme at the 1979 United Nations Conference on Science and Technology for Development held in Vienna. Unfortunately, the subject has become highly politicized around the terms of transfer, which makes it easy to ignore many of the more fundamental difficulties of ensuring the assimilation of processes devised for the industrial environment, in quite different situations. (The third assumption above). The real difficulties of transfer do not lie so much in the inadequacies of the present system as such, the machinations of the transnational corporations, or the inequities in the conditions of transfer, but in a failure on the part of both donors and receivers to appreciate that successful transfer is an exceedingly complicated socio-economic process with many facets and social conditions beyond the mere introduction of packaged processes and know-how. Above all it necessitates the existence in each country of an indigenous capacity for science, technology and industry, if imported processes are to be assimilated, take root and spread.

There seem to be three major requirements, then, for the effective transfer of technology from the industrialized to the Third World countries:

(1) Skill and sureness on the part of the planning, economic and other agencies of the less developed countries, in the selection from the vast number of technological possibilities available, of those items which are most essential and appropriate for their development, social as well as economic.

(2) Easy access to, and equitable conditions for, such transfers.

(3) The building up of a suitable infrastructure for science and technology in each case, to permit not only wise selection amongst the options, but also the capacity to modify processes and products to render them suitable for use with local materials and to respond to local cultural conditions, to ensure the assimilation of the new technologies and skills, both technical and managerial which come with them and hence to pave the way to future, general development.

The construction of an indigenous capacity for research and development, both within each of the developing countries and also shared to some extent regionally, seems to us to be the kernel of the development problem. The basic requirement is the realization that science and technology can only contribute significantly to development in the long term if they are regarded as inherent and essential elements in a socio-economico-political process and evolved in articulation with the productive system and that of education. A few developing countries such as Mexico and India are fully aware of the need to relate industrialization, in an organic sense, to the goals of society and of using science intimately coupled with the various sectoral developments. But this is not generally understood, hence the obsession with the terms of transfer. Research and development must be woven into the national fabric and not allowed to remain in an autonomous and isolated situation.

How, then, can such a capacity be generated? The facile approach is to propose the creation of new universities, to provide more research funds to those which exist, or again to found industrial research institutes, on the assumption that if there is more research, there will be more technology and hence more development. Each of these is excellent, if the new institutions are well conceived and integrated with the socio-economic system. Too often, however, they remain in isolation from the mainspring of national development and only breed frustrated scientists, ripe for the brain-drain. Third World universities also, can be isolated from the community they are designed to serve, outposts of learning remote from the local problems and preparing people of high quality for jobs that do not exist. This is doubly unfortunate, since many individuals in these universities have deep concern for national issues, but somehow find it difficult to get to grips with them, in the absence of any real relationship between the university and the economic and political hierarchy.

As to the industrial research institute; this can become a spearhead of innovation or be only marginally useful according to how it is related to, or isolated from, the total development situation. At the worst, it can be a mere alibi, a vaguely prestigious body, standing somehow outside the realities of the national situation. Experience shows that there is a tendency for such institutions, especially when set up and initially directed by foreigners, to wither away after an apparently promising start. Yet, there is a very real need for these institutions; the problem, once again, is how to link them with the on-going technological activity of the country and to ensure that the knowledge which they generate, or which they acquire by familiarity with advancing research elsewhere, is put to use.

There is thus no easy path to the creation of a vigorous scientific and technological capacity. It must be approached simultaneously from many angles—in the universities and technical schools, in agricultural institutes and extension services, in industry and in the public services—and must be supported by information services which can scan world developments, selecting and bringing to the attention of the authorities and to entrepreneurs, those elements of new knowledge which are significant to the needs of the society in question. This building-up process necessarily takes a long time and none of this can succeed unless there is general understanding on the part of politicians, public servants, the business community and the academics, of the essential need to create such an infrastructure, coupled with the other policies and activities of the nation. The creation of such a capacity for science and technology, together with an understanding of the nature of the technological innovation process must be the initial and major points of a science policy of those countries in early stages of development.

To sum up on this point; the technological needs of the developing countries are exceedingly diverse, but, in the main, fall into the following categories:

(1) The introduction of a mix of technologies designed specifically to meet the economic, social and cultural needs of each country, taking account, for example of employment needs and demographic trends, the availability of indigenous raw materials and energy sources, traditional skills and markets. Such a mix will normally include a nucleus of modern industrial development as a basis for future evolution. Usually this will be based on technology imported from the industrialized world, modified to take account of local materials and conditions. A wide range of established technologies exist which are freely available for the manufacture of products now imported, but even if free of patent restrictions, etc., they may necessitate the acquisition of difficult know-how.

(2) An applied research effort which might with advantage be undertaken

in cooperation with neighbouring countries with similar needs, aimed at evolving highly efficient but labour-intensive processes.

(3) Special attention to the needs of the traditional sector aimed at improving their tools, materials, methods and marketing.

(4) The constitution at both local, national and regional levels, of a scientific and technological competence to provide a sound and innovative basis for continuing development.

THE TRANSNATIONAL CORPORATIONS

The transnational corporations are at the centre of the controversy concerning technological transfer and its terms. Industry, including the state enterprises of the marxist countries, rather than government, is the main vehicle for the transfer of technology from the industrialized to the less developed countries and the transnational firms are of special importance in this connection, although their functions and aims are at present under suspicion in many quarters, often unfairly as the result of the behaviour of a minority. It is necessary here, therefore, to include some consideration of these enterprises, not only in relation to the development of the Third World, but more generally, since their size and sophistication, the extent of their research programmes, and their importance on the world market, give them a major role in world technological development.

Formerly, these firms were referred to as multinational. There are, however, few, if any, multinational firms in the strict sense of being financed and controlled on a truly international basis.

Most of them are enterprises capitalized and directed mainly from a headquarters in a single country, but operating simultaneously in many through their branches and subsidiaries. They

are undoubtedly the main agent at present for the transfer of technology and also management skills from the industrialized to the poor countries and also for the rapid diffusion of new processes and products between industrialized nations. As a consequence of this transfer they contribute to the increase of well-being and are an essential part of the world economic system. Being commercial enterprises, they aim at making profits by organizing production and selling products or services naturally to those who have the purchasing power to buy their wares. In many cases, they have made very big capital outlays in research and development to evolve new technologies and hence the transfer of these technologies, whether in the form of manufacturing plants or in the sale of patents and know-how, is an important element of amortization.

Being an important element of the economic system, the transnationals are involved in all the difficulties and contradictions of the unequal development of the world. Most countries aiming at industrialization are anxious to see some or many of the transnationals operating in their territories and hence these firms are at times in a position to play off one government against another, to probe for the best terms, and the power they exert often seems beyond the control of either the parent or the host countries. To anti-market politicians and those of many of the developing countries, the transnationals seem to be the apotheosis of capitalism and there is much suspicion concerning their motives and behaviour as a result of the activities of a few which appear to have abused their position by indulging in anti-social behaviour or even engaged in political activities in countries within which they operate.

The transnationals bring both advantages and disadvantages to the countries in which they are established. On the positive side they bring with them new technologies, rapidly and efficiently, also management ability and marketing skills; they are effective in training local cadres of skilled workers; they have great knowledge of international transactions and are fully aware of all the infrastructure and manpower needed for the type of manufacture they specialize in. The branches they establish are of an accepted world standard and can serve as pacemakers for industrialization in general.

The disadvantages of the transnationals stem mainly from their lack of permanent commitment to the objectives, both economic and social, of the host countries. The technologies they introduce are generally those which have been evolved for countries of the developed world, are highly capital-intensive and hence provide relatively little employment. They may thus produce goods which are not intrinsically important to countries at an early stage of development and by methods not appropriate to the employment and cultural ambitions of the host. In this way they tend to respond to the needs of the elites of the developing countries and much less to the welfare of the masses.

In view of the need to reduce wealth disparities between the rich and the poor countries and to take account of the changes implied in the trends towards the creation of a new international economic order, the transnationals are being forced to rethink their attitudes and policies. The suspicions to which we have referred necessitate a creation of a new image which it will take time to shape. The UN is at present working on a code of good practice for the transnationals. This may well prove acceptable to them, but it would be much better if they were to elaborate their own code and enforce it themselves. They will have to demonstrate clearly that they do have obligations to their host countries of a lasting nature, that they are politically neutral and socially responsible. Indeed, in the industrialized countries as well as in the Third World, industry will, as a matter of long-term self-interest, have to accept that it is an institution of society, with all the responsibilities which this entails, in addition to being profit-generating entities.

Many of the transnationals are well aware of these considerations and some are already concerning themselves with the elaboration of technological approaches suited to conditions in the Third World, attempting to maintain high levels of efficiency while allowing for a higher labour intensity. Others are undertaking research and development for their own purposes in the developing countries and in this way contributing to the building up of the local technical infrastructures. Again there is a greater awareness on their part, stemming from increased experience, of the long-term development needs of the host countries and appreciation in depth of the local cultural conditions which may be very different from those of the home base and necessitate different management approaches as well as modifications in manufacturing methods and products.

The transnational corporations will, at least in the immediate future, remain an important element in the process of technological transfer, but probably in very different circumstances from those of the past. It is necessary, but insufficient, that they should establish agreed codes of good practice to which they will voluntarily adhere, but they cannot be expected to carry their international social responsibilities to the extent that this would jeopardise their profit objectives, for example through the loss of their foreign investments in politically unstable areas before they yield profits. To encourage them to take such risks, it will be necessary, at the very least, to have guarantees from stable governments and presumably also from their parent company, against such risks. The basic requirement for successful technology transfer is to include the transnationals within a global strategic system based on the skill and resources of the richer, stable nations and not relying entirely either on good intentions or on the opportunity for profit. Behind this is the still more fundamental need to assist the Third World to become itself more technologically self-reliant.

IFIAS is presently carrying out a project on how the transnational corporations can optimally mobilize their resources and know-how in helping the LDCs to build a basis for sustained technological development. The project is specially focused on how the conflicting issues should be resolved to make this possible

CHAPTER 9

Industry and Employment — the Next Revolution

Present world trends in technology, in conjunction with the demographic and social factors, are likely to culminate within a few decades, in a general situation which, although fraught with many difficulties, holds promise for the evolution of societies very different from those of today and with new qualities and values. In this chapter, we shall stress the consequences of foreseeable technological development in the already industrialized countries, since it is in these that the first, massive effects will be felt, although the realities of world interdependence will quickly communicate the consequences of such developments to countries at all stages.

With regard to the Third World, we have already noted that the present demographic trends and structures are expected to result in a relatively greater increase in the work-force than in the total of the population. In order to intensify and extend agriculture so as to provide food for the growing population, a considerable proportion of the inflated work-force will, in any case, have to be absorbed by the food production sector. Nevertheless, the main hope of achieving a substantial increase in the living standards of many countries, still resides in industrialization. The target of the United

Nations, that the industrial production of the less developed countries should reach 25% of the world's total by the year 2000, is probably not realistic, but considerable increase is to be expected with important repercussions on the markets of the highly industrialized nations. Undoubtedly, one of the main objectives of the developing countries will be to produce jobs as well as products. This leads us back to our earlier opinion that industrial policies for many sectors in these countries should not automatically emulate the high manpower productivity approaches of the traditional industrial system.

For most of the presently industrialized countries, a series of quite different issues are likely to arise. If the present low levels of fertility persist, there will be a considerable shrinking in the proportion of the total population in the active work force. This may well, as we shall see shortly, be welcomed on employment grounds, but will bring its own difficulties and have deep repercussions on industrial and technological policies, especially for the resource-poor nations of the second category in the classification presented in Chapter 3. It will mean, for instance, that a much higher proportion of the population will be elderly than at present, which will put great strains on the health and welfare services, resources for which will have to be provided from the work product of the shrinking proportion of active people. This will, of course, be alleviated to some extent by the smaller numbers of children entering school, an effect already beginning to be felt in some countries. However, considerable pressures on the educational system are likely to arise from quality, rather than quantity, considerations, while, as we shall see later, demands for leisure education, recycling and the cultural needs of populations partly relieved from the burden of work, will necessitate fundamentally new and probably not inexpensive transformation of education and training.

The shrinking of the active labour force in the industrialized countries would necessitate, in terms of constant production levels, therefore, a product achieved by smaller numbers, i.e. higher manpower productivity achieved by means of technological innovation and presumably by the production of goods of an advanced type for the world market, of high added value in terms of skill and scientific and technical content.

For the resource-poor, industrialized countries, technological innovation needs will be especially great. Dependence on external supplies of raw materials and energy is likely to orient industrial development in countries such as Japan and those of Europe, both East and West, towards miniaturization, the invention of products and processes involving minimum quantities of materials for their construction and of energy in their manufacture. Thus one must expect in these countries, rapid development of industries such as those of electronics and pharmaceuticals, considerable investment in the recycling of metals and the conversion of wastes, production of goods with a long operational life and stress on modular design which will allow the rapid and easy replacement of faulty or worn components. Such a transforma-

tion will not be easy within economic policies based on market stimulation of demand such as we have today. Indeed, for countries at present highly industrialized and lacking in energy and raw material resources, the final and major resource is the skill and enterprise of their people

All this suggests that such countries should already, in view of the length of the educational cycle, be making strenuous attempts to improve education and training at all levels, to increase their research and engineering capacities and to evolve a social system to provide equality of opportunity for education. Prospects for such an evolution are by no means dim, but, as is the case for countries at all levels of development, it is important that the political and intellectual leaders are fully aware of the changing needs and, therefore, ready to plan for industrial and social transition well in advance. We cannot repeat too often that wherever there is reliance on technological, social and educational innovation to provide for future needs, the inherently long lead time of these processes demands a perspective of at least 20-30 years in the planning process. It is essential that all should appreciate the need to avoid the temptation to sacrifice long-term stability and prosperity for ephemeral short-term gains.

THE NEW TECHNOLOGIES

We now turn from the demographic to the technological prospects and our main argument here is that spectacular advances in technology, influencing the primary, secondary and tertiary sectors of the economy are so great and so immediate that it should be possible in the not too distant future to provide all the resources needed by an industrialized country, including those for health, education and welfare, not merely by the reduced labour forces which are to be expected, but by only a fraction of these. Thus the real problem in such countries is likely to be, not the insufficiency of the young and active in an ageing population, but of providing employment, or rather satisfying occupation, to large populations partially relieved of the necessity to spend the greater part of their waking life in work.

There seem to exist, therefore, conditions for a second Industrial Revolution, with economic and human prospects as deep as, and much more immanent than, were those of the first. To master this new wave of promise will demand exceptional wisdom on the part of the leaders of society and understanding on that of people generally, since deep societal transformation will be involved. An immediate question must be raised at this point—how will the Third World, which has as yet only fractionally absorbed the consequences of the first Industrial Revolution, be able to apply the fruits of the second?

Of the new technological openings we shall mention here only two, the development of microeconomics and especially the applications of the microprocessor and new lines of biological advance.

The microprocessor, a product of solid state physics, has evolved in close association with the computer. It is a development of the circuit miniaturization process which has been advancing for several decades. It is able to incorporate on a half-inch long sliver or chip of silicon, tens of thousands of transistors with their associated circuitry. It may cost as little as $20 and a single-chip microcomputer can be bought for as little as $100. The first electronic digital computers, introduced at the end of the second world war, were bulky installations containing as many as 7,500 relays and switches, 18,000 vacuum tubes and 70,000 resistors. A later generation was greatly reduced in size by the invention of the transistor. The equivalent today, based on the silicon chip is 300,000 times smaller, 10,000 times faster, much more efficient in its use of power and, at the same time, much more reliable. This development goes far beyond the mere miniaturization of electronic

gadgetry; it is a breakthrough which will have enormous impact on all sectors of the economy and, eventually, on the daily lives of all human beings. Amongst the initial applications of silicon chip technology, the following already exist or are to be expected quickly:

> the electronic watch and calculator;
> the personal microcomputer;
> improved functioning of the internal
>   combustion engine;
> fuel efficiency;
> domestic appliances of many kinds (e.g.
>   microwave ovens; the domestic
>   robot);
> information selection and retrieval;
> novel transportation systems and traffic
>   control;
> computer-aided design;
> the automated office and the automated
>   factory;
> industrial process control;
> environmental monitoring;
> medical diagnosis and prosthesis;
> automatic translation and
>   interpretation;
> the tele-video conference;
> computer-aided educational systems;
> electronic mail and other communi-
>   cation systems.

In fact, the microprocessor makes possible the inexpensive introduction of a brain—computer elements and memories—in the whole range of manufacturing and consumer instrumentation devised by man, while it articulates easily with other developing technologies such as satellite communication and glass-fibre optics.

Of course, such a revolutionary development will have many social and human impacts, as yet only dimly foreseen. It will tend to increase greatly the interdependence of individuals and nations; it could make for an ever greater complexity of institutions and societies, already becoming so complex as to be virtually unmanageable; like other technological developments it will increase the fragility of society; it can provide the perfect basis of surveillance and control of the individual by "big brother" dictators and societies; it could abolish personal privacy. Nevertheless, the potential economic and competitive advantages of this event are such, that mankind will certainly not be able to resist the benefits of its applications. Seldom before, has there been a stronger subject for technology assessment to foresee the cultural and social, in addition to the economic, consequences of a development which is too significant and too dangerous to be left to the vested interests of single groups, or indeed of single nations.

Further, although at first sight less dramatic, lines of advance are likely to arise in coming decades from biological research, particularly from molecular biology and enzyme science. Genetic consequences may be expected first in agriculture, but the possibilities of genetic engineering on human behaviour and breeding are already raising deep ethical doubts both in scientists and amongst the lay public. Enzyme technology, in putting micro-organisms to work to provide products for human consumption, is as old as man himself; fermentation to alcohol was one of the primitive inventions, concurrent with the shaping of the first tools. Now, however, genetic manipulation offers the prospect of a much wider range of bio-conversions and has the advantage that, although the science may be extremely sophisticated, its technological application is relatively very simple.

There is, at present, a considerable development of bio-resource technology for the conversion of wastes, agricultural, animal and human, into foodstuffs and energy. Most of this is at a relatively primitive scientific level, but is capable of considerable development. This approach is often seen, and indeed, often cultivated as a sort of counter-culture technology, or as a means essentially for the alleviation of poverty in rural areas of the Third World, but this is not necessarily so, especially if developed within the perspective of the total biomass system. The widespread use of biogas in China and some other East Asian countries, shows that there is general significance in the approach, especially when combined with other possibilities such as algal and fish culture, the use of waste heat, employment of new enzymatic approaches, full use of agricultural wastes, the use of new varieties of fast-growing leguminous trees and supplemented by simple solar devices. One of the features of this approach is that it is not very capital-intensive and, as we have seen, although capable of using advanced biological knowledge, the applications are relatively simple and capable of easy assimilation in traditional economies and cultures.

IFIAS activities on self-reliant development using such an approach include village development, based on the total and integrated use of the available biomass for the production of food and energy and also a novel development of a biological fuel cell for the direct conversion of hydrogen and methane to electricity. It should not be concluded, however, that the bio-resource approach is exclusively a matter for remote and primitive communities; it will no doubt develop initially and rapidly at the village level, but has great potentialities for large scale exploitation in the urban environment, especially in relation to the total and productive use of sewage and municipal wastes, as energy becomes scarcer and more expensive. Manipulation of the genes of micro-organisms so as to make possible the enzymatic production of a vast range of chemicals may also open the way to new industries.

INDUSTRIAL AND TECHNOLOGICAL POLICIES

The great possibilities within the next generation of technological development, together with the complex social and cultural consequences which they entail, raise questions concerning the governance of technology, not necessarily its detailed control, but at least its general direction in terms of social and not merely economic desirability. The future directions of technological change are thus a legitimate, and even an essential, concern of governments and must be considered seriously in the decisions of corporations working within the general framework of national policy. The direction of technological policy will be determined in part by national objectives and the external forces of general world trends, and also by potentialities for desirable exploitation presented by new discoveries of science, arising either within the country or imported from other parts of the world. Identification of technological probabilities necessitates a competence in government for technological forecasting, with a rather long-term perspective and also, as we have suggested, for technology assessment. Few governments are sufficiently knowledgeable concerning the detailed operations and considerations of industrial development or capable of assessing the significance of scientific trends, so that one has to envisage the cultivation of a new type of tripartite relationship between government, industry and science, if the best interests of a nation are to be served.

Forecasting the direction of future scientific achievements is particularly difficult, because of unexpected discoveries and discontinuities which are bound to arise in any creative research, from the emergence as it proceeds, of new facts, phenomena and concepts which modify its direction and tempo in mid course and may throw up quite new technological possibilities or obstacles. On the contrary, it should not be impossible to identify the general direction, although not the details, of technological development a few decades ahead, since the innovations on which such developments will be made, will be based mainly on scientific knowledge already uncovered.

However, *technological forecasting* cannot be made on the basis of technology alone, but will be influenced also by economic, social and political events which, in modifying national objectives, will modify also the demand for, and, to some extent the direction of, new technology.

In the free-market economies, industrial corporations with their large research units and awareness of world scientific development are well placed to take primary advantage of new technical possibilities although not as yet sufficiently concerned with their social and cultural consequences. Even in countries such as the United States and Japan, however, governments are increasingly involved in ensuring that some of the more obvious technological hopes are encouraged with sufficient intensity and vigour. With regard to microprocessors for example, it is in the United States and Japan that the biggest efforts are being made. It is estimated that the US government is expected to provide between five and eight hundred million dollars for such purposes in the next five years, while Japan has programmes calling for six hundred million dollars in four years. In contrast, the German allocation for approximately the same purpose and period is about forty million dollars only, while France has allotted about one hundred and forty million dollars for the microelectronics industry.*

TECHNOLOGICAL TRENDS AND THEIR INFLUENCE ON WORLD DISTRIBUTION OF INDUSTRY.

The forecasting of changes in the pattern of industry is even more uncertain than that of technology as such, since many other factors operate including the cost and availability of raw materials and energy, demographic trends, entrepreneurship, fiscal policies, management-labour relations and also general political con-

*For a completion of this theme, see Keith Pavett, Technical Change: the Prospects for Manufacturing Industry, *Futures,* August 1978, p. 283.

siderations. On the global level particular uncertainty is involved according to whether or not the concept of the New International Economic Order becomes a reality and the extent to which the Third World countries succeed in their plans for industrialization.

However, even without taking into account the longer-term consequences of the microprocessor `development, some shorter-term trends in the pattern of manufacture seem probable. In the presently industrialized countries it seems likely that changes in market demand will lead to a decline in household consumer durables as a consequence of the approach to saturation, but this is likely to pick up later when the new generation of "intelligent", computer-brained equipment begins to appear. There may also be a lessening of output of synthetic (especially petrochemical) materials and agricultural chemicals as such production tends to move towards the raw material sources, many of which are in the Third World, for economic reasons, high transportation costs and general world development considerations. Similarly there should be a trend for the beneficiation of minerals and primary metallurgical extraction to take place near to the ore bodies, since high energy costs will make it increasingly absurd to transport enormous amounts of useless rock (gangue) in which a small proportion of metal is embedded, enormous distances to the industrialized countries and this should be of considerable benefit to the mineral-producing countries of the developing world.

High energy costs may also depress and cause profound design modification in automobiles and other equipment, but encourage products which save energy or provide the means of using soft energy sources. Examples are insulating materials and products, solar panels and other collecting devices, photo-electric equipment, windmills, heat pumps, etc. Similarly, the industrialized countries will en-courage the materials recovery and recycling industries and encourage the manufacture of goods of modular construction and long operational life. The same trend will favour the development of the nuclear industries (despite social opposition resulting from recognition of the dangers inherent in nuclear power generation) and also (if the coal option for the energy of the future is taken up) of mechanical mining equipment, and of plant to produce oil and gas from coal and coal-based aromatics and other chemicals.

Industrialization in the Third World will include a high degree of manufactures to provide import substitutions. It will also seek to produce products for export, initially textiles, plastics, consumer goods, bulk synthetics and intermediates, and a wide range of simpler conventional machinery and machine tools, possibly also automobiles. If the period is one of general economic depression in the industrialized world, protectionist restrictions on the part of some governments and trade unions are to be expected. Such countries should realize, of course, that rapid industrialization in the Third World should be accompanied by growth at home, in many of the capital goods sectors, alloy steels and specialist chemicals both in the heavy, fine and pharmaceutical branches of the industry. However, it has to be recognized that industrialization in the developing countries may necessitate a considerable change in industrial *structure* in the developed nations.

The longer-term prospects resulting from the microprocessor revolution are, initially at least, unfavourable to the countries of the Third World. At quite an early stage, the silicon chip will transform most of the existing electronic products and render unnecessary much of the delicate assembly work which has proved so beneficial to countries such as Korea, Taiwan and Hong Kong. Moreover it will eventually remove the one marginal advantage of all developing countries, namely relatively cheap labour, so that the highly industrialized countries will be tempted, through fully-automated factories, to build, for example, quite new types of textile industries which could be extremely competitive.

EMPLOYMENT

Employment consequences of some of the trends we have outlined could be very profound, although they also open the road to a quite different type of society in which the *work ethic* is unlikely to be anything like as important as it has been through the industrial development era. Ever higher levels of manpower productivity which will be required for competitive effectiveness and the great expansion of electronic development and control will tend to suppress jobs, although employment possibilities in some of the quite new directions we have indicated may go some way to compensate for this. Unless, however, continuously expanding markets can be found, there is a fear that technological unemployment may become endemic. Indeed, we may be reaching in some countries, the situation feared by the machine wreckers and Luddites at the beginning of the Industrial Revolution, where the replacement of men by machines becomes a reality. So far, of course, such a situation has been held off and made to seem absurd, by the fact that technological development has, throughout nearly two centuries, lowered the cost and increased the value and volume of industrial production to the extent of creating new *mass markets* of consumption both in the countries where it takes place and, through export, abroad. High rates of economic growth which have been characteristic of our times have thus created new jobs continuously over the decades to the extent that a number of European countries have had to attract very large numbers of *" guest workers"* from abroad to enable them to maintain production levels. If it is not possible to continue this process and maintain high growth rates indefinitely, for reasons of materials and energy cost and scarcity, as well as of saturation of demand, massive unemployment is unevitable unless there are fundamental changes in the nature of the industrialized societies, including attitudes to work. This possibility will have to be a major consideration in the planning of future technology. There is likely, initially at any rate, to be a bitter conflict between the need to maintain high levels of employment and that to innovate and increase manpower productivity for economic survival. This will be a particularly difficult problem for the European countries with few natural advantages, and for which, therefore, innovation and high productivity will be essential. These problems may also hit those countries of South East Asia, which have recently achieved considerable success in industrialization and growth. A considerable element of this success has resulted from electronic assembly for which local skills have proved to be particularly apt. The advent of the microprocessor is a grave threat to the continuation of this.

Many claim that the surplus labour from high productivity industry will be absorbed by the tertiary sector. This is somewhat improbable; experience of recent years indicates that as consumers become more prosperous, they do not, as had been assumed, spend higher proportions of their incomes on "services" in contrast to "goods". In practice they purchased more cars, to the detriment of public transportation, domestic equipment to replace domestic help which had become scarce and expensive, and television and hi-fi instead of going to the theatre, cinema or concert. Thus the individual tended to replace labour-intensive services by capital-intensive mechanical and electrical equipment. Of course, public sector growth in health-care, welfare and education has syphoned off much income to the services and has created huge government bureaucracies in many places.

It would be a mistake, therefore, to assume that the *service sector* will, in the future, automatically absorb the surplus manpower and womanpower which may become redundant in a high-productivity and electronic dominated economy. Indeed, many service activities may be even more influenced than the manufacturing sectors by the microprocessor revolution, especially in the early phases and the great bureaucracies, in any case unpopular, will tend to fade away. Employment in communications, transportation, banking, commerce and large areas of the public service is likely to be seriously affected, unless productivity in these sectors is held at an artificially low level to maintain jobs and this will be difficult if the economy is to be efficient and competitive. There will therefore be an aggravation of the old dilemma of how to maintain high levels of employment in the face of rapid technological advance and economic needs, with a growing awareness that more jobs and services will have to be supported by the competence of industry to supply the over-all resources.

It is, however, just on this issue that the greatest possibilities for social betterment lie. The present prospects for the application of new technologies, especially in microelectronics, widely and wisely used, are so great, that in the future it should be possible to create all the resources needed by an advanced, industrialized society, including those for defence, education, health and social welfare, through a work force, proportionately much smaller than that of today. This is no new dream; it has been the hope of the visionaries since the latter years of the eighteenth century. Indeed, in the view of the present author, many of the basic views of that time, including those of Malthus, of the machine wreckers and of the fathers of the Industrial Revolution who foresaw that the applications of the new science and mechanics could lead to the abolition of poverty and the arising of a new and better

society, diverse and contradictory as they seemed at the time, were essentially correct, but premature by a couple of centuries. Furthermore it should be possible to reconcile them.

The possibility of the new stage in the development of technology producing the necessary resources, with a minimum of human labour and with less consumption of energy is now high and is capable of allaying the fears and achieving the visions we have just alluded to. But to do this will require a transition of society which would be fundamentally revolutionary and will have to be determined by humanistic criteria. Its achievement would require understanding, wisdom and foresight on the part of the leaders of society, creative partnership between government, industry and science and a high degree of awareness on the part of the public generally of the possibilities and difficulties of the transition. Decision on these matters must come within the next few decades, if it is to come at all; either we seize upon the new possibilities which are presented by the inexorable flow of events and face up to the social adjustments inherent in their acceptance, or else the industrial societies will degenerate through inertia, social strife and a lack of courage and confidence. The countries most likely to make the transition to the new type of society are those which are particularly well integrated and socially cohesive. Here, Japan, one of the leaders of microelectronic research and application, comes to mind, having prepared for the "information" revolution for at least ten years already and being particularly skilled at social adaptation.

At the heart of the difficulty are our present concepts of work, employment, unemployment and *leisure,* with the heavy and historical values which attach to these words. To achieve the transition to a new and equitable industrial society and to make possible the fulfilment of the individual as well as the harmony and efficiency of society, the focus of concern will have to change from that of employment in the traditional sense to occupation in the larger view and with a reassessment of the *work ethic*. The occupation of the individual will have to be seen broadly as comprising a proportion of productive employment as it is understood today, but presumably occupying a much smaller proportion of the time of the individual (later entry, earlier retirement, shorter hours of work), together with one or more subsidiary occupations of a craft, artistic or educational nature, in addition to leisure in the normal sense. The "economically productive" element of occupation would include periods freed for educational recycling and for the deepening of the subsidiary occupation by the acquisition of new techniques, practice and experience gained under a teacher. The secondary occupations would be unpaid, but would usually have to be organized to a certain extent, with tools and instruction provided directly or indirectly by the State. Education would have to be modified considerably to allow for both the primary and secondary occupations and would be conceived in terms of life-long learning; its initial and formal stage would have to be of high quality to provide the skills and understanding necessary to allow industry to provide the national resources to support the total system. Unemployment in the present sense with its pejorative and demoralising image would no longer exist. We have indeed already entered the age of leisure, without realizing it and without having adjusted our structures, attitudes and economic processes to allow for it. Whether the average individual has the inner resources to live without the discipline of work is another question.

These are no utopian visions, but the possibilities within the grasp of contemporary man. The technological potentials for their achievement already exist; whether there is the will and understanding to exploit them to the benefit of all mankind is another matter.

CHAPTER **10**

Emerging Patterns of Change

Having concluded our summary of the trends of change in a number of the important areas of human activity, we now come to the general summary of the situation of the Planet Earth and of the individual, political and institutional reactions to the current trends.

As we stated initially, today's world is constructed on the basis of a very successful technology, increasingly derived from scientific discovery. Thus material prosperity, unequally and inequitably distributed as it is, has grown enormously since the second world war and with it all the manifestations of the massive technology which has made it possible. However, as Kenneth Boulding puts it, "baddies come with goodies; each treasure chest is also a Pandora's Box". The enormous gains have heaped up enormous problems, so that affluence has produced its counterpart in dissatisfaction and alienation; vastly improved health and hygiene have eliminated diseases and contributed to the population explosion; exceptional economic growth seems to entail a wasteful consumption of planetary resources to the disadvantage of our successors, threats to the environment and a neglect of human values other than the strictly material. And we are facing the new challenges of scale, complexity, change and uncertainty, with institutions which

are static and archaic, with political systems and ideologies concerned mainly with the pursuit of quantitative growth, and obsessed by the immediate and economic theories which no longer seem to work.

What, then, can we conclude about the state of the planet? Its health is not too good and there are a number of ominous symptoms. The "patient" should, perhaps, be put on the danger list or at least kept under constant observation. The condition is, however, as yet far from hopeless, but return to health will only be possible after a number of remedial measures and a change in the way of life, away from the present frenzied growth tempo. Unfortunately the diagnosis of this complicated case is far from complete and a much more thorough examination of the "patient's" metabolism and functioning is required before the remedies can be confidently prescribed. Brutal surgical intervention is not recommended for the moment, but it may have to be envisaged as the condition develops. This is, of course, simply the subjective view of the present diagnostician; many would take a more serious view.

In the period since the writing of the first edition of this essay, the world situation can hardly be said to have improved. True there are some signs of a slowing down of fertility rates in a few countries where this is most pressing, but the general prospect of a greatly increased world population still persists. Little progress has been made towards the abolition of poverty or in the better distribution of income in the poor countries, and the New International Economic Order seems as distant as ever. In the industrialized countries inflation has not yet been effectively controlled, high levels of unemployment persist, and youth unemployment (socially, particularly undesirable) is difficult to eliminate; economic growth has slowed down in most countries—but for the wrong reasons, and economic difficulties are still regarded as temporary. On the political side, there has been much talk about disarmament, but the overkill capacity of the major powers increases, while the poorest nations pile up armaments they can ill afford, and wars which are termed minor, but which involve great loss of life and widespread hardship and disease, are in progress in many places. Violence and terrorism have been rampant, even in countries which appear strong and stable.

One of the disappointments has been the seemingly interminable discussions at the Law of the Seas Conference and the unilateral action by a number of important countries to extend their "economic limits" 200 miles from the coastline. Although an international ocean "regime" is envisaged to control the exploitation of the oceans and their beds beyond the greatly extended national limits, this division of space in the "last frontier", which was hitherto international, invites the spread of conflict and, with the new possibilities of exploring the ocean riches, the powerful and technologically competent will be favoured as usual, at the expense of the poor and underprivileged, unless special arrangements can be made.

On the positive side, the one major development has been a noticeable deepening and spreading of public understanding of and concern for the world situation. Innumerable con-

ferences, debates, broadcasts and publications have exposed the various elements of the world *problématique*. The creation of a public awareness of the nature and gravity of the problems facing mankind is critically important. It is all too easy to blame governments for the difficulties of the moment, but politicians can only act in terms of general consent. The public is naturally concerned with difficulties which can be immediately recognized and which impact on the individual. Further off, although perhaps much more serious, problems are not seen as of immediate menace and are hence of minor concern to the voter. Furthermore, many of the measures which may be necessary to establish long-range world harmony will be disagreeable and disturbing in their short-term effects and hence politically unpopular, and it is the exceptional statesman who will risk his popularity and the coherence of his party by facing up to the longer-term issues which are likely to be aggravated and currently critical, only after he is out of office. While public awakening to the gravity of these matters is encouraging, it is as yet quite insufficient to make possible the necessary political action. Perhaps the most fundamental need of the moment, therefore, is to inculcate in the public mind in all countries an understanding of the world situation and the need for a longer horizon of concern. Some, but by no means all the political leaders are aware of the critical importance of these considerations and not all are well served with regard to the significance of the mounting difficulties. For this reason there is need, both nationally and internationally, for a scanning mechanism to identify and inform about the mounting difficulties.

We have already stressed the need for institutional innovation. In many countries, governments have already started to experiment with the creation of new types of institution. In the Netherlands, for instance, there is a recently formed Scientific Council for the Study of the Problems of Government, attempting to look rationally and systematically on many of the current problems and suggest modifications in structures, policies and procedures. We have already mentioned the Secretariat for Future Studies attached to the office of the Prime Minister and Parliament of Sweden and also some of the Canadian institutions. It is interesting to note that the Science Council of Canada, with government finance, has recently completed a series of studies on the Conserver Society, which attempt to suggest modifications in life-style and economic behaviour to meet some of the problems we have discussed. These have attracted much interest in a country which seems to the rest of the world to be particularly well endowed by nature in its resources; not only are they being discussed by the general public, but also by industry. These experiments with new institutions are, however, but a tentative and cautious beginning.

On the international level there is also much movement. It is true that the United Nations is an assembly of the sovereign states of the world and has to balance and attempt to harmonize the usually conflicting views and aims of its members. Nevertheless, through its series of conferences on global issues of the last few years and planned for the next—Environment (Stockholm 1972), Population (Bucharest 1974), Food (Rome 1974), Habitat (Vancouver 1976), Water (Argentina 1977) and Science and Technology for Development (August 1979)—it has helped in the delineation of the problems and in bringing them to the attention of the world public. Many feel, however, that these huge meetings are over-politicized and indulge mainly in pussyfooting, lacking courage to face up to the main issues and often hardly daring to mention them. This is, to some extent, true, but they are valuable in their emphasis on major problems and in softening up positions to allow more realistic approaches later. It should be noted also that the UN has responded to the concern regarding the future by creating, within its Institute for Training and Research (UNITAR), a "Com-

mission for the Future" under the distinguished presidency of Monsieur Phillipe de Seynes.

The present call for a New International Economic Order may well be naive and rhetorical, but it represents a determined demand for change in the world economic system on the part of the majority of nations of the world, mainly but by no means exclusively those of the Third World, and places responsibility for continuation of the *status quo,* squarely on the shoulders of the great powers, which they will find it very hard to ignore. This new movement implicitly rejects the simple model, whereby the nations are classified into three categories, the advanced countries of the market and of the marxist worlds and the underdeveloped countries, with income redistribution seen in aid terms as a kind of self-protecting charity from the rich to the poor. The new Order would be based on the creation of a greater degree of self-reliance within each country and on interdependence within a limited world, of a whole spectrum of countries at different stages of development, vastly different possession of natural resources, varying environments and potentialities for food production and greatly differing densities of population, each with their particular needs and their particular contributions to the whole.

Both nationally and internationally there is a great proliferation of bodies, mostly private, but some semi-official, devoted to study or propaganda concerning specific problem areas such as population, or to the totality of the world situation. Some of these bodies are essentially scientific, others are politically oriented and often extremist; some are sensible, others fanatical or hopelessly idealistic. However, there seems to be emerging a network of serious non-governmental organizations of a new type, dynamic in their approach and to some extent working in concert. The Club of Rome is one of these, which has acted as a gadfly to complacency through its widely distributed reports, the second of which gives, at last, the beginnings of a practical method to enable decision-makers to weigh the importance of the various elements in a complex problem area and to foresee the consequences of possible alternative policy scenarios. Pugwash, the first of these bodies, has already been influential in its field and is now endeavouring to extend its scope of interest. The International Institute of Applied Systems Analysis at Laxenburg in Austria, is active in developing sophisticated quantitative approaches to the understanding of many of the world problems. The United Nations University has made an all too modest start. The developing countries have formed their own organization to study the world problems—the Third World Forum. IFIAS itself is slowly shaping a flexible network of multidisciplinary research on some of the most difficult elements of the *problématique*. Even the European Common Market has completed a comprehensive study of its needs and those of its members for long-term projections, appreciation of future trends and technology assessment in its Europe plus Thirty exercise.

None of these initiatives is sufficiently forceful or comprehensive by itself, but together they represent a new surge of serious concern for the state of the planet and they do comprise a radically new institutional approach in contrast to that of the older and more static organizations.

CHAPTER 11

The Way Ahead— Some Pointers to Survival

Although the planetary problems are both complicated and menacing, we are far from concluding that the situation is hopeless. There are some grounds for optimism in the gradual progress towards understanding as to how the global system really operates, of the specific dangers which loom ahead, and of where the limits to human expansion and the barriers to human survival lie. This growth of awareness is inevitably the first, but only the first, step in the long and painful process of resolving the predicament of mankind.

There are, of course, many scenarios of the future development of society. Their very range and diversity—they run from the wildly optimistic, science fiction variety to the starkly apocalyptic—is extremely confusing to the average thinking person who feels himself in an uncertain suspension between a future technocratic heaven and a universal Götterdämmerung. In our view there are many options still open to mankind and both extremes are possible, although neither one is probable. Undoubtedly, new scientific discovery has much to offer man, both in increasing his understanding of the universe, his societies and his own nature and, through its application as

technology, to the construction of a world which can provide decent conditions of life to all its inhabitants. Success here probably depends less on the genius of scientists yet to be born, than on the wisdom of the people and their leaders in making a large series of wise decisions as to the type of world they wish to see and hence as to the directions of application of the new knowledge. Science, as we continually stress, is not an autonomous activity which will spontaneously determine the nature of the planet in the future, but a marvellous means for the generation of knowledge which can be used for good or evil. This is not to say that science—and particularly social science—is value-free, but to underline the old distinction between knowledge and wisdom. The knowledge is already there and can be greatly increased; the basic problem is how to cultivate the wisdom to use the knowledge. There is certainly no single panacea.

There are a whole series of limits to human expansion and to the ever greater rhythm of human activity. Whether we are approaching these limits is a matter of good judgement based on sufficient information. No doubt, many of the limits can be pushed back by wise policies and advancing technology.

The first group of limitations which we begin to see are becoming known as the *outer limits.* These are the material constraints of an inevitably bounded planet—availability of materials and energy at reasonable cost, the toleration of the environment to absorb the waste products of man's activity, without irreversible damage, the presence of sufficient productive soil and of water to grow the necessary food and industrial crops and thus also the population level. These are the variables considered in the Club of Rome's controversial study, *The Limits to Growth.* With competent management of the world's resources, intelligent cooperation between the nations, restraint, foresight and wise use of technology, it should certainly be possible to maintain high standards of material existence for many years to come. The key issues cluster around the uncertainties as to the level at which world population will level off and around the availability of sufficient, cheap and clean energy. As we have seen, the next fifty years will be critical with regard to both of these uncertainties and will certainly entail a difficult period of transition from waste to conservation. With regard to the outer limits we can be cautiously optimistic, but great vigilance, foresight and possibly sacrifice on the part of many, will be necessary for a smooth passage through the transition. Most of IFIAS projects are dealing with outer limits problems.

Then we come to the *inner limits;* those of society and politics. The Club of Rome itself has stated that the outer, material, limits are unlikely ever to be encountered, because in front of them lie a series of more fundamental barriers, economic, social, political, managerial and, eventually, in the very nature of man.

Man is a social animal and his biological evolution has been accompanied by an evolution of his social habits. From the emergence of small groups of families and larger tribes to share the burdens of hunting, food gathering and mutual protection, through the settlements of a systematic agriculture, the emergence of villages and cities, to the nation states of today, humans have continually adjusted their relations with one another: sharing tasks, banding together for protection against enemies, yielding individual privilege and independence of action for security and material betterment. However, in the past, the societal adaptations have been very gradual, while today society must modify so as to survive in the technologically dominated world of interdependence between the nations, in the span of one or two generations.

The man-made world in which we find ourselves, is no longer that of the village, the city or the country which our fathers knew, but a complex of artificial systems in transportation, defence, production, aerospace, communication, information, data storage and retrieval which have radically transformed our planet. The tragedy is that our social and cultural competence has hardly advanced, so that society is in great unbalance. Instead of riding triumphantly on the chariot of the material revolution, as he had deceived himself into imagining, man finds that he is out of control, that his power is treacherous and can lead to self destruction. In addition, there seems to be no shared ethic of the species; man is still hopelessly divided into tribes, each striving for dominance and only dimly aware of, or having the willingness to admit, the common human need to work together for survival and to reap the enormous harvest which his knowledge can provide.

There would seem, therefore, to be a desperate need to redress the balance and to develop the social and cultural attributes of humanity until they match its material power. It is doubtful if this can be done within the existing ideologies of the world, but yet adapt he must, if man is to survive as a species.

The inner limits then are very real, diffuse,

ill-marked and difficult to grapple with. Once again we must conclude that the beginning of a solution must lie in awareness of the evil. Our educational systems are ill adapted at present to preparing the young for life and work in the world which is emerging. What is needed is a complete reappraisal of the learning process and not just of the formal stage of schooling.

Still more intangible and fundamental are the third group of potential limits, which we may call the *innermost limits,* in that they reside in the very nature of the human individual. This is not the place to discourse on the nature of man with all its contradictions which has been the subject of analysis of all the religions and philosophies since the dawn of man's historical existence. Nevertheless, there are acutely relevant points to be made between the human condition and the state of the planet.

While human ingenuity and effort have changed the world utterly, the individual man in his wonderful, gigantic and monstrous creation, seems relatively unchanged since ancient times, with all the old motivations and aspirations, idealism and pettiness of his remote ancestors. There is little evidence that human wisdom has increased over the last four millennia during which information and power have mushroomed.

Modern and relatively affluent man is, however, living in a quite different emotional and mental environment from hitherto. Freed from degrading poverty, he no longer needs or responds to bread and circuses provided by the State to keep him docile as in the past. He has often lost faith in the traditional religions and is no more disciplined by the hope of heaven or fear of hell. The political processes have in many cases lost their appeal or seem a mere game; they appear corrupt, self-seeking and irrelevant. Even social reform loses its attractions as the more crass forms of poverty disappear. He is worried and unsure as to the meaning and aim of existence. He is beginning to be aware at last of his position as a member of a biological species and as such realizes, if he thinks at all, that he can no longer be served by the processes of organic evolution. These are too slow to benefit him and the race will destroy itself, long before the superman can evolve, either by the bang of nuclear annihilation or the whimper of social disintegration. The question is, therefore, whether *homo sapiens,* as presumably the only species aware of the nature of his existence and mortality and lacking, it seems at present, a compulsive *raison d'être,* can learn in time to shape his own destiny.

But here the difficulties begin. So many of the attributes built into his nature over the ages and which have permitted him to survive, to dominate all other creatures and to displace weaker races are utterly inappropriate, and indeed exactly the opposite of what is required to provide him with the wisdom he so desperately needs for the harmonious development of human society. The motive forces for self-evolution are greatly different from those of organic evolution. Egoism and basic selfishness, greed, aggressiveness, striving for power and dominance over others; such characteristics have served him well in the past and have been the basic forces in his successful struggle against nature through the survival of the fittest. Although, as man became more and more a social and cooperative animal, many of the grosser manifestations of these attributes became softened or sublimated, they are still ineradicably built into the nature of man. The same qualities that the individual possesses, are also operative in a collective sense in the State. The egoism of the individual, projected to the level of the nation, is chauvinism with all its suspicions and urges towards domination of other countries and races. Most international negotiations are conducted on a basis of immediate self-interest and with little regard to longer-term consequences, to say nothing of general global consequences or the welfare of future generations.

These negative characteristics do not, of course, represent the totality of human nature. Man also has his ideals and aspirations; he is devoted to his family, his community and his nation—extensions of his own ego. He is devoted to the construction of utopias, is capable of altruism and self-sacrifice, and enjoys indulgence in charity. Man was always a Faust-like creature and his double standards seldom worry him. Furthermore, as we have remarked, in the process of evolution man has acquired many useful social characteristics, a willingness to sacrifice certain elements of his individual freedom for collective security and the possibility of living harmoniously and prosperously with his neighbours. Indeed, it is in social evolution that much of the hope of survival of the race resides—in that and in his marvellous capacity for adaptation, which is one of his greatest strengths.

What then is to be done? There are two fundamental approaches, the external, to which most of this book is devoted, and the internal. The latter would concern the development of the individual, aiming at an evolution of consciousness and the overcoming of the more brutal aspects of human egoism. This has been at the basis of most religions, or at least of their mystic elements, since ancient times, but although many techniques of self-development are claimed, there is little evidence that they have ever achieved generalized success. Nevertheless, this approach has a certain appeal to many young people in the West today. While every effort should be extended to find means of improving the nature and motivation of the individual, it would be naive to expect quick results in a situation which demands immediate action.

Assuming then, the continuation of individual and collective egoism, the greatest hope would seem to lie in educating that egoism towards its own long-term self-interest. It is too much to expect that through a widespread and deeper education leading to a general understanding of the nature and complexities of the human condition, that people will be willing to espouse as a major motivation, the survival of the human race; nevertheless, through such an understanding, it ought to be possible to persuade the individual to defer some of his immediate material ambitions and the gratification of immediate desires, at least to the extent of providing decent conditions of life for his children and grandchildren—his extended ego. If this could be achieved, it would at least give a breathing space to allow other developments and plans.

The three sets of limits are, of course, intimately related in the being and behaviour of the individual in his society, so that it will be necessary to attach together the outer and the inner, taking account of the constraints within man himself. It would be presumptious, if not irresponsible, to attempt to present here a blueprint of what should be attempted. We are still far too ignorant of many of the factors of the situation, to be sure of how to act. Yet, it is necessary to indicate a few essential lines of action, required to establish, as it were, a holding position, to enable the world to assess the needs more precisely and to elaborate a sure strategy to face the perils of uncertainty. Even the following simple suggestions will appear vague and utopian in view of the inevitable political disagreements and power struggles arising from collective egoism. They are, however, indications of a way ahead. The need to grope towards the series of wise decisions for their establishment is urgent and here one should note the conclusion of Professors Mesarovič and Pestel in their report to the Club of Rome, entitled *Mankind at the Turning Point,* on the basis of computerised calculations, which indicate the enormous costs, both in money and human suffering, of delay in tackling the contemporary problems of population increase, food provision and energy.

Amongst the many actions required to contain the situation, the following are especially advocated:

(1) Information and Understanding

This is basic and critical. There is a primary need to spread and deepen understanding of the present difficulties and potential dangers within the world system, throughout the whole population of the planet and especially among the decision-makers, local, national, and international. This will have to be done by a variety of means: through the formal educational system, by radio, television, the printed word, parliamentary debates, discussions in the schools, in the board rooms of corporations, and in the streets. The present book is but a modest contribution towards the creation of a network of efforts which will have to permeate society and become a world movement, if it is to achieve significant results in influencing individual and collective behaviour. Especially in the democratic societies, political leaders cannot take vital decisions without popular support and popular understanding. Most of the measures required by the situation are bound to be unpopular and no statesman could survive if he attempted to promulgate them without general understanding of their necessity. However, in such a situation wise leadership is essential and it is necessary that a few of the most far-sighted of the political leaders should sound the alarm and support overtly the growth of public understanding of the issues at stake.

The basic problem here is within the educational system itself which requires profound reform and a new approach to the process of learning, if the new generation is to grow up with a sense of reality concerning the world into which they are thrown.

(2) World Solidarity

As a consequence of an enhanced understanding of the global difficulties, there must be a drive for solidarity in facing them, encouraging a common recognition in all people of their common situation as members of the human race. Uniting in the face of danger should be an elementary attainment. However, history shows that disintegrating civilizations in the past have seldom achieved it, often because they were unaware of the gravity of the perils they faced, until it was too late. If, however, the dangers of the contemporary world can be shown as common to all humankind, there may be some hope. Most international negotiations start from the differences which separate the nations. Ervin Laszlo, in his book *Goals for Mankind,** has shown that there is, in fact a very large measure of common objective and purpose within the declared objectives of nearly all the power groups of the world, nations, ideological groups and religions. It is of vital importance to begin discussions based on the body of agreed objectives and to attempt to enlarge their area, rather than to stress the difficulties at the outset. Only thus can a solidarity based on wise common self-interest have real substance.

(3) World Watch

In view of the rapid development of many of the contemporary problems and the largely unidentified cross-impacts between them, there is a need to provide to all peoples a service which continuously scans and monitors the world situation, giving warning of impending dangers before they descend, following the energy and raw materials position, population growth, migration, food availability, climatic anomalies, etc. Such a "World Watch" would

*E. Laszlo *et al., Goals for Mankind,* Dutton, New York, 1977.

also help, no doubt, to identify also, new scientific possibilities as they emerge, pointing out their significance in relation to our understanding of the "world *problématique*" and for attack on its constituent problem elements. Such an institution would have to be supported by governments but, to be effective, would have to be objective and independent, free from political and ideological influence. It could be conceived as the international centre of a network of specialized institutions, both governmental and independent, national and international. Such a body would not only provide a service to all governments and all people, but could greatly help to inculcate a general prospective attitude in other institutions. In a way IFIAS may be considered as a first step toward such a "World Watch" function.

(4) The New International Economic Order

This still nebulous conception is far from becoming a reality and it is not regarded with much favour by the presently rich countries and especially by the superpowers. The concept is, nevertheless, gathering substance and becoming a familiar idea. The need for a new system based on justice and equity is self-evident, if we are to attain a harmonious world, but the measures required to achieve it are still unclear. The whole concept will have to be rethought in terms much broader than the merely economic, which is but one strand in the tangle of the *problématique.*

(5) Alternative Strategies and Policies

We have stressed the need to evolve new approaches to the management of scale, complexity, change and uncertainty which is an art, still unknown, but which must be cultivated. Much too little is known about the process of decision-making and with the growing recognition of the interactions between problems and

sectors, much more sophisticated approaches are necessary if the multi-variant problems facing the nations are to be solved. The human brain is capable of dealing with very few variables at a time and most decisions are based on the intuitive qualities, experience and sense of political feasibility on the part of those who make them. Doubtless these attributes always will, and always should, be determinative; but a much deeper consideration of the factual basis of situations is required than in the past, if unexpected and unwanted (counter-intuitive) consequences are to be avoided. Much can be done, even on the basis of existing techniques, to explore and test out the consequences of ranges of alternative options, before a decision is made to promulgate a particular policy.

(6) The World Food Situation

Those countries with the largest and most quickly growing populations and greatly in need of increased agricultural output are in the tropics; yet, most of the most important agricultural research to date has been for the benefit of temperate agriculture. There is great need to intensify research on many aspects of agriculture in the tropics. Very important developments are taking place in the various international research institutes for particular crops and they need increased support as do many national agricultural centres. Every effort should be made to intensify agriculture where its products are most needed and great importance must be given, not only to genetic and other agricultural research in the narrow sense, but also to water availability, management and efficient use, to preservation and improvement of productive soils, reforestation and the like.

However, it is not likely that domestic agriculture in many places will be able to keep up with population growth, at least in the short term, or be sufficiently viable to cope with climatic variation, hence those countries possessing possibilities for still further agricultural expansion, should be ready with contingency plans. In particular, greater efforts should be made to build up world grain reserves in years of good harvest, to be available over the "lean years" and, at the receiving end, improved storage facilities and measures of pest control are necessary to eliminate the enormous wastage by insects and rodents.

(7) Population

Increased and generalized understanding of impending world problems, and especially of the population-food-energy complex, should incite countries to establish firm policies for their demographic evolution and to ensure that these are fully understood by the local populations and voluntarily put into effect. In each case, these policies should be devised in terms of the specific national conditions, including prospects for water availability, industrialization, and health requirements. It would be useful if countries would undertake studies on the carrying capacity of their land surface, taking into account (where appropriate) the contributions which might be made from their economic zones of ocean. These should make possible the demonstration of the probable standards of living which would be possible at different levels of population.

All countries, including the rich, industrialized nations should begin collective discussion of the consequences of present demographic trends in terms of changing economic patterns, pressures towards migration, employment needs, political factors and social and cultural aspects. Special consideration should be given to the problem of the necessary expansion of the infrastructure to meet the vastly increased populations, how this can be financed, and its economic implications for countries of all types.

(8) Energy and Materials

Long-term world policies for energy and materials should be devised quickly in view of the probability of a period of shortfall in the coming decades and the need to develop non-traditional sources of energy as rapidly as possible so as to shorten the transition period. Political awareness of the necessarily long lead time of research and development is essential, as is the need to ensure that future energy should be "clean" and thus not threaten the environment and climate. The aim should be to achieve a diversity of sources of energy supply and to avoid reliance on single ores and materials. Efforts are also required to encourage conservation of energy and materials, to utilize wastes, to devise efficient methods of recycling and to design products of long life.

(9) Economic Growth

National long-term policies for economic growth should be reviewed in the light of social and ecological consequences of rapid growth and must stress quality aspects, the need for material and energy conservation and a more equitable distribution of wealth. There is special need to ensure that the technology of the future should be socially acceptable, both in ecological terms and in the humanization of work, and hence mechanisms of technology assessment should be created and national science policies modified to give greater attention to social and cultural aspects.

(10) Urban Problems

In view of rapid population growth and increased industrialization in many Third World countries, the prospects of massive urban development are threatening. Before it is too late, strategies of industrial location should be devised to ensure that the mistakes of the already industrialized countries are not repeated and that industries are placed with suitable dispersion to ensure that too great and hence socially undesirable concentrations of people are avoided and also to bring greater harmony between rural and urban populations, as well as providing greater opportunities for cash incomes in purely agricultural areas. In countries at present highly industrialized and possessing great cities, problems of urban renewal are pressing and should be tackled in terms of improved life styles and the need for energy conservation.

(11) Disarmament

This is, perhaps, the most pressing of all the problem areas of the *problématique*. International disarmament negotiations should be accelerated and given a new dimension by the realization of the influence of the waste of energy, materials and human resources through armaments, on the other pressing problems of our times. Special attention should be given to the arms trade as such and to the building up of excessive military capacity by poor countries, already in a desperate economic position. It is realized, of course, that disarmament can only be achieved with a lessening of tension between the nations and in this connection our suggestions concerning solidarity are relevant.

(12) Research and Development

National and international research and development policies should be reassessed and priority given to the exploration of long term ecological dangers, the need for increased food production, the actualization of non-traditional energy sources, health and many of the other topics mentioned above. In particular, much research is required into the problems of decision-making and the exploration of alter-

native strategies and policies. To meet many of the uncertainties which face us, it may well be necessary, as a world, and also as a national, insurance policy, to devise many alternative technological options to be brought to productive use as needs become clearer. This will entail many contingency developments up to the engineering prototype or chemical pilot plant stage, ready for rapid introduction of new production, if required as a result of energy changes, ecological needs or the unavailability of particular materials. Such activities, as with all insurance, would be costly, but much could be done internationally or between groups of neighbouring countries on a cost-sharing basis. New methods of international technological cooperation are required, involving programming in common, undertaking of elements of the work by existing institutions, universities and firms, most appropriate in each case, and sharing of the results. Encouragement should be given to research, pure and applied, in the social sciences as an important ingredient in the transdisciplinary attack on global problems. Particularly, there is need for much exploration in the science of economics, in view of its difficulties in the present situation and of the need to take into account the many intangible factors which influence national development and which are not always possible to include in monetary terms. There is especial need for a closer linkage of economic and social policies.

Doubtless there are many other grave problems of a social, political or cultural character which demand to be studied and resolved, but if the above were explored with the seriousness and weight of effort they deserve, the holding situation might be achieved and the world given a little breathing space to face the more basic difficulties.

Many will argue that a full and frank exposure of the dangers at present facing the world, would only generate fear and possibly hopelessness and apathy on the part of millions, with strongly disruptive consequences. This is a matter which merits deep consideration. But the situation is far from hopeless; enormous possibilities exist for the future of mankind which has always responded to challenges. Stress must be laid on the positive aspects; man has never before faced such diverse alternatives and is likely to flourish through knowledge rather than to languish in ignorance.

Index